To Karen, Michael
Happy reading!
Gil Friedman
Feb '03

D0722989

Love Notes

Quotations from the Heart

Compiled by Gil Friedman

YARA PRESS
Arcata, California

Previously published as *A Dictionary of Love.*
Revised version including 11 new categories.

Yara Press
1735 J Street
Arcata, CA 95521
Phone: 707-822-5001
Fax: 707-825-8112
E-mail: gil@humboldt1.com
Web page: www.yarapress.com

ISBN 0-913038-00-8

Painting on cover, a detail from Pierre-Auguste Renoir's *Danse à la campagne (Country Dance),* courtesy Musee d'Orsay, Paris, France.

Photo of painting: © Photo RMN – Harvé Lewandowski

Cover art: Lynn Lozier-Hannon

This book is printed on acid-free paper, which reduces the amount of sulfuric acid released into the atmosphere.

PERMISSIONS

Every effort has been made to trace and contact copyright owners. If there are any inadvertent omissions in the acknowledgements, I apologize to those concerned and will make corrections in any future editions. Since a single copyright page cannot accommodate all the permissions and copyright notices, this page and succeeding permission pages constitute an extension of the copyright page. The extracts listed below are reprinted with kind permission of the following:

(Permissions continued on page 206)

CONTENTS

D

E

M

N

P

R

S

T

U

V

W

INTRODUCTION

Over 2,500 years ago the Buddha observed that two things can break your heart: one was not to get your heart's desire, and the other was to get it. In no field does this seem to apply more than in our love life.

Many modern marriages and relationships are like fortresses under siege. Those who are in want out, and those out, in. In the past, many such couples met, fell in love, experienced initial bliss, started a relationship and married. Then they started to experience the decay of their relationship and love over a period of years. They went through various stages, such as the "seven-year itch," before the love, and the relationship, died, whether the couple stayed together or not. Today this process can take place in a couple of months or even over a weekend.

With so many relationships not living up to initial expectations, most everyone would like advice on the next step in his or her love life, or whether to take any step at all. Advice, however, can be a tricky matter. As the German proverb goes, advice is something the wise don't need, the foolish won't take, and everyone is overstocked with; and, as the 17th-century Frenchman La Rochefoucauld said in his book *Maxims,* "Old people like to give good advice since they can no longer set bad examples."

Some who give good advice have been temporarily incapacitated from setting bad examples. For example, honor and gentleness toward women were never more idealized than in the tales of King Arthur's Knights of the Round Table. The original English version of this myth was in a book, *Morte d'Arthur,* written by Thomas Malory while in jail for extortion, looting a monastery and two counts of rape.

Good examples can also cause problems, as Mark Twain pointed out: "Few things are harder to put up with than the annoyance of a good example."

Yet one is still tempted to read and think about what many of the great philosophers, thinkers and writers have thought about love. In some technical fields, last year's technology might be outmoded today, but, as far as love goes, what someone said 2,000 years before Christ might be just as valid now. Jo Coudert observed in *Advice from a Failure:*

> There is nothing old under the sun; each of us must learn again, from the beginning, for ourselves; but the learning process can be hastened and deepened and solidified by a personal and creative borrowing of the insights of other people. The exactitude of a phrase someone else uses may sum up an idea hitherto dimly groped for. A writer's point of view may open a region which would otherwise go unexplored. The rightness of an observation may be so remarkable that an approach to an event or person may never be the same again.

This is a book of maxims, aphorisms and short excerpts about love with 202 categories in an alphabetical order, from "Action and Love" through "Wounds and Love," by more than 300 authors. These quotations record the myriad observations on the universal subject of love. The reader can locate any aspect of love in a matter or seconds and read what a writer, philosopher or famous personality has said about it.

I do not expect the reader to agree with every quote; I don't. Each one, however, is provocative and will exercise and hopefully amuse the reader's mind. Quotes placed beside each other sometimes appear totally contradictory, but the reader will find upon close examination that seeming inconsistencies help pinpoint how we really feel about various issues.

Whether one reads just a few of the sayings or all of them, there is much to enjoy and mull over in this book. I hope you enjoy reading it as much as I enjoyed putting it together.

Action & Love

Every man feels instinctively that all the beautiful sentiments in the world weigh less than a single lovely action.

James Russell Lowell

Admiration & Love

To love is to admire with the heart; to admire is to love with the mind.

Theophile Gautier

We always love our admirers, but not always those whom we admire.

Francois de La Rochefoucauld
Maxims, 1665

Adventure & Love

We are all functioning at a small fraction of our capacity to live fully in its total meaning of loving, caring, creating and adventuring. Consequently, the actualizing of our potential can become the most exciting adventure of our lifetime.

Herbert Otto

Advice on Love

For you to ask advice on the rules of love is no better than to ask advice on the rules of madness.

Terence
The Eunuch, 161 BC

Listen to no one who tells you how to love. Your love is like no other, and that is what makes it beautiful.

Paul Williams
Das Energi, 1973

No one can give you better advice than yourself.

Anonymous

Affection and Love

Our affections are our life. We live by them; they supply our warmth.

Anonymous

Intellect strips, affection clothes.

Ralph Waldo Emerson

A heart without affection is like a purse without money.

Monderstann

Where there is room in the heart, there is always room in the house.

Mae

At the end only two things really matter to a man, regardless of who he is; and they are the affection and understanding of his family. Anything and everything else he creates are insubstantial; they are ships given over to the mercy of the winds and tides of prejudice.

Richard F. Byrd
Alone, 1938

Be yourself. Especially, do not feign affection. Neither be cynical about love; for in the face of all aridity and disenchantment it is perennial as the grass.

"Desiderata"

The affections are not so easily wounded as the passions, but their hurts are deeper and more lasting.

Charles Dickens
Barnaby Rudge, 1840

It is part of the human condition to long for the unexpressed. The simple word of genuine thanks, the modest sign of appreciation, the sincere expression of affection really make a difference in our lives. We cannot explain why these little signs mean so much to us. But the fact is that a word of thanks for some small thing can transform our day.

Joseph Simons and Jeanne Reidy
The Risk of Loving, 1968

Love is too pure a light to burn long among the noisome gases that we breathe, but before it is choked out we may use it as a torch to ignite the cozy fire of affection.

Jerome K. Jerome
The Idle Thoughts of an Idle Fellow, 1899

Age and Love

Love is the word used to label the sexual excitement of the young, the habituation of the middle-aged, and the mutual dependence of the old.

John Ciardi

From birth to age eighteen, a girl needs good parents. From eighteen to thirty-five, she needs good looks. From thirty-five to fifty-five she needs a good personality. From fifty-five on, she needs good cash.

Sophie Tucker

A young man loves the first woman who flatters him.

Honore de Balzac
As quoted in *The Wisdom of Balzac*, 1923

The heart that loves is always young.

Greek proverb

A man is only as old as the woman he feels.

Groucho Marx

Younger men are more supportive and a lot less demanding, and they also have more time for their relationships.

Cher

When a person does not give up on sex, sex does not give up on the person.

Gabriel Garcia Marquez

All one's life as a young woman one is on show, a focus of attention, people notice you, you set yourself up to be noticed and admired and then, not expecting it, you become middle-aged and anonymous. No one notices you. You achieve a wonderful freedom. You can move about, unnoticed and invisible.

Doris Lessing

Oh to be 70 again!

Oliver Wendell Holmes, Jr.
(On the occasion of his passing a pretty girl
on the street at the age of about 85.)

Alchemy and Love

The only transformer and alchemist that turns everything into gold is love. The only magic against death, aging, ordinary life, is love.

Anais Nin
The Diary of Anais Nin, Vol. 4, 1971

Ambition and Love

Children, you must remember something. A man without ambition is dead. A man with ambition but no love is dead. A man with ambition and love for his blessings here on earth is ever so alive. Having been alive, it won't be so hard in the end to lie down and rest.

Pearl Bailey

We frequently exchange love for ambition, but never ambition for love.

Francois de La Rochefoucauld
Maxims, 1665

Anger and Love

The anger of lovers renews the strength of love.

Publilius Syrus

Anger wishes all mankind had only one neck; love, that it had only one heart.

Jean Paul Richter

When you see a married couple coming down the street, the one who is two or three steps ahead is the one that's mad.

Helen Rowland

When you communicate to other people in a way that honors their deeper being, you always feel better about yourself. You may have noticed that when you got something off your chest by expressing anger or hurt, you often felt worse afterwards. At the very least, there is a sense of incompletion. You cannot leave a situation until you have done so with love. Those situations you leave in anger will be there for you to resolve in the future. It may not be with the same person, but you will create another person and a similar situation to allow you to resolve it with peace and love.

Sanaya Roman
Living with Joy, 1986

Anxiety and Love

Anxiety is love's greatest killer. It makes one feel as you might when a drowning man holds onto you. You want to save him, but you know he will strangle you with his panic.

Anais Nin

Apologies and Love

Apologizing is a way of keeping current with your relationship, of making sure that the two of you aren't loving through a window so fogged by old complaints that it's impossible to see or be seen clearly by one another. Apology consists of three essential parts: stating your crimes by name, saying you're sorry, and asking to be forgiven. It differs radically from defensiveness. When we are defensive, we become lawyers for our own case: "I did it because . . . " "I didn't mean to do it," "He, she, or it made me do it." "It isn't what it appears to be," "It's all in your mind," "It was no big deal." All these defensive postures have the effect of muddying the emotional waters. . . . Defensiveness is a way of keeping a relationship problem going. Apology gives closure, opening the path to forgiveness and a new beginning. Most of us can never apologize enough. Apology ---- when it is genuine and come from the heart ---- is one of the quickest healers of any-sized rift, the perfect bandage for every wound in a relationship.

Daphne Rose Kingma
True Love: How to Make Your Relationship
Sweeter, Deeper and More Passionate (1991)

Arithmetic and Love

The arithmetic of love is unique: two halves do not make a whole; only two wholes make a whole.

Jo Coudert
Advice from a Failure, 1965

Love, and you shall be loved. All love is mathematically just, as much as the two sides of an algebraic equation.

Ralph Waldo Emerson

In the arithmetic of love, one plus one equals everything, and two minus one equals nothing.

Mignon McLaughlin

And in the end the love you take is equal to the love you make.

John Lennon and Paul McCartney
Abbey Road, 1969

Attachment and Love

One must not become attached to animals: they do not last long enough. Or to men: they last too long.

Anonymous

Attitude toward Love

Love is not primarily a relationship to a specific person, it is an *attitude,* an *orientation* of *character* which determines the relatedness of a person to the world as a whole, not towards one "object" of love. If a person loves only one other person and is indifferent to the rest of his fellow man, his love is not love but a symbiotic attachment, or an enlarged egotism. Yet most people believe that love is constituted by the object and not by the faculty. Because one does not see that love is an activity, a power of the soul, one believes that all that is necessary is to find the right object --- and that everything goes by itself afterward. This attitude can be compared to that of a man who wants to paint but who, instead of learning the art, claims that he has just to wait for the right object, and that he will paint beautifully when he finds it. If I truly love one person, I love all persons, I love the world, I love life. If I can say to somebody else, "I love you," I must be able to say, "I love you in everybody, I love through you the world, I love in you also myself."

Erich Fromm
The Art of Loving, 1956

Attraction and Love

We attract hearts to the qualities we display; we retain them by the qualities we possess.

Scad

Corporal charms may indeed gain admirers, but there must be mental ones to retain them.

Colts

Aversion and Love

Aversion gives love its death wound and forget-fulness buries it.

Jean de La Bruyere
Characters, 1688

Barriers to Love

When the outside world sets up a barrier against your love ---- drastic as a monastery wall or the ban of exile ---- then thank God if she loves you in return, even though you have neither sight nor sound of her. For love has lit a candle for you in the dark forest of the world. And little matter that you put it to no immediate use; he who dies in the desert possesses his dear home none the less for being far away from it.

Antoine de Saint-Exupery
The Wisdom of the Sands, 1950

Beauty and Love

He who desires a lifetime of happiness with a beautiful woman desires to enjoy the taste of wine by keeping his mouth always full of it.

George Bernard Shaw
Man and Superman, 1903

The average girl would rather have beauty than brains because she knows that the average man can see much better than he can think.

Anonymous

The expression a woman wears on her face is far more important than the clothes she wears on her back.

Dale Carnegie

It's better to be looked over than overlooked.

Mae West

What a strange illusion it is to suppose that beauty is goodness.

Leo Tolstoy

A beautiful woman is a picture which drives all beholders nobly mad.

Ralph Waldo Emerson

All women think they're ugly, even pretty women. . . They all find fault with their figures . . . Even models and actresses, even the women who you think are so beautiful that they have nothing to worry about do worry all the time.

Erica Jong

A witty woman is a treasure;
A witty beauty is a power.

George Meredith

In so much as love grows in you, so beauty grows. For love is the beauty of the soul.

St. Augustine

A man can feel his heart touched by certain women of such perfect beauty and such transcendent merit that he is satisfied with only seeing them and conversing with them.

Jean de La Bruyere
Characters, 1688

Belief and Love

Love eagerly believes everything it wants to.

Jean Racine
Mithridate, 1673

Who so loves
Believes the impossible.

Elizabeth Barrett Browning
Aurora Leigh, 1856

Not to believe in love is a great sign of dullness. There are some people so direct and lumbering that they think all real affection must rest on circumstantial evidence.

George Santayana
The Life of Reason: Reason in Religion, 1905-1906

The Bible and Love

If I speak in the tongues of men and of angels, but have not love, I am only a resounding gong or a clanging cymbal. If I have the gift of prophecy and can fathom all mysteries and all knowledge, and if I have a faith that can move mountains, but have not love, I am nothing. If I give all I possess to the poor and surrender my body to the flames, but have not love, I gain nothing.

Love is patient, love is kind. It does not envy, it does not boast, it is not proud. It is not rude, it is not self-seeking, it is not easily angered, it keeps no record of wrongs. Love does not delight in evil but rejoices with the truth. It always protects, always trusts, always hopes, always perseveres.

Love never fails.

And now these three remain: faith, hope and love. But the greatest of these is love.

1 Corinthians 13:1-8, 13 (NW)

Beloved, let us love one another; for love is of God; and everyone that loves is born of God, and knows God.

He that loves not, knows not God; for God is Love.

John 4:7,8

Bitterness and Love

Bitterness imprisons life; love releases it. Bitterness paralyzes life; love empowers it. Bitterness sours life; love sweetens it. Bitterness sickens life; love heals it. Bitterness blinds life; love anoints its eyes.

Harry Emerson Fosdick
Riverside Sermons, 1958

Blindness and Love

Love, though proverbially blind, is often prone to see something which has no existence whatever.

E.F. Benson

Love is not blind ---- it sees more, not less. But because it sees more, it is willing to see less.

Julius Gorden

Passion may be blind; but to say that love is, is a libel and a lie. Nothing is more sharp-sighted or sensitive than true love, in discerning, as by instinct, the feelings of another.

D. H. Davis

Books and Love

Those who love reading have received one of the greatest gifts God can offer. They can become acquainted with, friends of, and even intimate with all the great minds the world has created and will create through the written word.

Gil Friedman

The primary and fundamental purpose of an education is to inculcate in the students the love of reading and books. With this love the students can then spend the rest of their lives educating themselves and derive many hours of pleasure. An education that fails to do this is merely a trade school, regardless of what degree the students receive, or how much money they subsequently earn. Moreover, the great irony is that the students so short-changed never realize just how badly they have been cheated and what a richer life they could have had if this love of reading had been inculcated in them.

Gil Friedman

Some people make love, and some people write books about love, and a few do both.

Gil Friedman

A home without books is like a kitchen without food.

Gil Friedman

Brilliant Achievement and Love

My most brilliant achievement was my ability to be able to persuade my wife to marry me.

Winston Churchill

Brotherly Love

When the seeds of brotherly love take root in the hearts of people, wars will cease.

Paramahansa Yogananda

Celebration and Love

One should only celebrate a happy ending; celebrations at the outset exhaust the joy and energy needed to urge us forward and sustain us in the long struggle. And of all the celebrations a wedding is the worst; no day should be kept more quietly and humbly.

Johann Wolfgang von Goethe

Change and Love

We are not the same persons this year as last; nor are those we love. It is a happy chance if we, changing, continue to love a changed person.

W. Somerset Maugham
The Summing Up, 1938

Love is more afraid of change than destruction.

Friedrich Wilhelm Nietzsche
Miscellaneous Maxims and Opinions, 1879

The belief that relationships change only bilaterally is the most significant reason why relationships are so difficult to change. Acceptance of your unilateral capacity to alter significant relationships is the most powerful step you can take in beginning the process of change in your experience of life. The risk is accepting whatever the resultant change in the other may be.

Thomas Patrick Malone and Patrick Thomas Malone
The Art of Intimacy, 1987

Personality change follows change in behavior. Since we are what we do, if we want to change what we are, we must begin by changing what we do, we must undertake a new mode of action. Since the import of such action is change, it will run afoul of existing entrenched forces which will protest and resist. The new mode will be experienced as difficult, unpleasant, forced, unnatural, anxiety-provoking. It may be undertaken lightly but can be sustained only by considerable effort of will. Change will occur only if such action is maintained over a long period of time.

Allen Wheelis
How People Change, 1973

Children and Love

Children begin by loving their parents. After a time they judge them. Rarely, if ever, do they forgive them.

Oscar Wilde
A Woman of No Importance, 1894

The best brought-up children are those who have seen their parents as they are. Hypocrisy is not the parent's first duty.

George Bernard Shaw
Man and Superman, 1903

Men love their children, not because they are promising plants, but because they are theirs.

Halifax

If you have never been hated by your child, you have never been a parent.

Bette Davis

A man finds out what is meant by a spitting image when he tries to feed cereal to his infant.

Imogene Fey

Praise the child, and you make love to the mother.

William Cobbett

Familiarity breeds contempt ---- and children.

Mark Twain

Love is presently out of breath when it is to go uphill, from the children to the parents.

Halifax

The first half of our lives is ruined by our parents and the second half by our children.

Clarence Darrow

The fundamental defect of fathers is that they want their children to be a credit to them.

Bertrand Russell

Children aren't happy with nothing to ignore,
And that's what parents were created for.

Ogden Nash
Verses From 1929 On, 1952

The child who is loved can love himself. And the ego that is loved is a strong ego.

Jo Coudert
Advice from a Failure, 1965

Eye contact is crucial not only in making good communicational contact with a child, but in filling his emotional needs. Without realizing it, we use eye contact as a primary means of conveying love, especially to children. A child uses eye contact with his parents (and others) to feed emotionally. The more parents make eye contact with their child as a means of expressing their love, the more a child is nourished with love and the fuller is his emotional tank.

Ross Campbell
How to Really Like Your Child, 1978

For fear of flattering, these dreadfully sincere people go on side by side with those they love and admire, giving them, all the time, the impression of utter indifference. Parents are so afraid of exciting pride and vanity in their children, by the expression of their love and approbation, that a child sometimes goes sad and discouraged by their side, and learns with surprise, in some chance way, that they are proud and fond of him. There are times when the open expression of a father's love would be worth more than church or sermon to a boy; and his father cannot utter it ---- will not show it.

Harriet Beecher Stowe

Choice and Love

It is a mistake to speak of a bad choice in love, since, as soon as a choice exists, it can only be bad.

Marcel Proust
Remembrance of Things Past, 1913-1927

Love is the free exercise of choice. Two people love each other only when they are quite capable of living without each other but *choose* to live with each other.

M. Scott Peck
The Road Less Traveled, 1978

Generally the woman chooses the man who will choose her.

Paul Geraldy

Commitment to Love

Loving people is a commitment to holding a high vision of them, even as time and familiarity take their toll.

Sanaya Roman
Living with Joy, 1986

Common Sense and Love

This is the worst of life, that love does not give us common sense, but is a sure way of losing it. We love people, and we say that we are going to do more for them than friendship, but it makes such fools of us that we do far less, indeed sometimes what we do could be mistaken for the work of hatred.

Dame Rebecca West

Companionship and Love

And in the end there is no desire so deep as the simple desire for companionship.

Graham Greene

Passion may be absent from a life and still the individual manages, but let companionship be absent and the life is insupportable. Friendship is the enduring joy. It is not spectacular nor intriguing nor electric, which is perhaps why it is not used to sell soap or automobiles, why it figures only passingly in our literature, why no symposia are held to examine it. So much the better that it is a neglected topic; we deserve one area free of exploitation, corruption, and self-conscious exploration. But we should not be feinted, by the silence of the professional, into underrating its importance in our lives. Add meaningful and satisfying work to meaningful and satisfying companionship, and no life, no matter how devoid of success, can fail to be a success.

Jo Coudert
Advice from a Failure, 1965

Having someone wonder where you are when you don't come home is a very old human need.

Margaret Mead

Completion and Love

Love is never complete in any person. There is always room for growth.

Leo Buscaglia
Love, 1972

Couples combine in relationship in order to complete themselves. It is not a random process....We select with astonishing precision that other person who can teach us what we need to know to be a more whole human being. We pair with the difference we need in order to complete ourselves.

Thomas Patrick Malone and Patrick Thomas Malone
The Art of Intimacy, 1987

What we really see in our loved one ---- what we really are attracted to ---- is what we have not yet opened to in ourself. The beauty and wholeness which has always been within us we first project onto our beloved. Then we yearn to be with our beloved and enter full-swing into the cosmic dance of relationship. Finally, the dance awakens us to the remembrance of our original wholeness ---- and holiness. However, unless we enter fully the dance of love, we might remain on the sidelines yearning for that which we already have.

Barry Vissell and Joyce Vissell
The Shared Heart, 1984

Compliments and Love

Compliments are the verbal nourishment of the soul. They generate self-esteem, and in a very subtle way create a person in the full spectrum of his or her essence. Compliments invite the person who is complimented to embrace a new perception of him or herself. And just as layers and layers of nacre form a pearl over an irritating grain of sand, so compliments collect around us, developing us in all our beauty.

Daphne Rose Kingma
*True Love: How to Make Your Relationship
Sweeter, Deeper and More Passionate,* 1991

Concern and Love

Love is the active concern for the life and growth of that which you love.

Erich Fromm
The Art of Loving, 1956

Conjugal vs. Romantic Love

Romantic love can very well be represented in the moment, but conjugal love cannot, because an ideal husband is not one who is such once in his life, but one who every day is such.

Soren Kierkegaard

Cooking and Love

Cooking is like love. It should be entered with great abandon or not at all.

Harriet Van Horne

There is one thing more exasperating than a wife who can cook and won't, and that's the wife who can't and will.

Robert Frost

Courtship and Love

A woman begins by restricting a man's advances and ends by blocking his retreat.

Oscar Wilde

Cancel the wedding ---- but renew the courtship.

Alexander Drey

If men acted after marriage as they do during courtship, there would be fewer divorces and more bankruptcies.

Frances Rodman

A chap ought to save a few of those long evenings he spends with his girl till after they're married.

Frank McKinney Hubbard

In a courtship the heart beats so loudly it blocks out the sound from the mind.

Bern Williams

Dancing and Love

All the ills of mankind, all the tragic misfortunes that fill the history books, all the potential blunders, all the failures of the great leaders have arisen merely from a lack of skill at dancing.

Moliere

Great dancers are not great because of their technique; they are great because of their passion.

Martha Graham

As to male dancers, there are not good ones or bad ones, but as in love itself, only strong and weak leads.

Gil Friedman

Dancing is safe sex's finest moment.

Gil Friedman

Death and Love

There is a wealth of unexpressed love in the world. It is one of the chief causes of sorrow evoked by death; what might have been said or done but that was never said or done.

Arthur Hopkins

No one should be allowed to die before he has loved.

Saint-John Perse

The great tragedy of life is not that men perish, but that they cease to love.

W. Somerset Maugham
The Summing Up, 1938

The confrontation with death ---- and the re-prieve from it ---- makes everything look so precious, so sacred, so beautiful that I feel more strongly than ever the impulse to love it, to embrace it, and to let myself be overwhelmed by it. My river has never looked so beautiful. . . . Death, and its ever-present possibility, makes love, passionate love, more possible. I wonder if we could love passionately, if ecstasy would be possible at all, if we knew we'd never die.

Abraham Maslow
(in a letter written while recuperating from a heart attack)

Love, like death, changes everything.

Kahlil Gibran
Spiritual Sayings of Kahlil Gibran, 1962

The loss of love is a terrible thing. They lie who say that death is worse.

Countee Cullen
On These I Stand, 1947

We are never so defenseless against suffering as when we love, never so helplessly unhappy as when we have lost a loved object or its love.

Sigmund Freud
Civilization and Its Discontents, 1930

We bury love,
Forgetfulness grows over it like grass:
That is the thing to weep for, not the dead.

Alexander Smith

Love knows not its depth till the hour of separation.

Kahlil Gibran
Spiritual Sayings of Kahlil Gibran, 1962

Decay of Love

It's not love's going that hurts my days
But that it went in little ways.

Edna St. Vincent Millay

Love dies only when growth stops.

Pearl S. Buck

When we have actually ceased loving a person,
it is impossible to love them a second time.

Francois de La Rochefoucauld
Maxims, 1665

If two people who love each other let a single
instant wedge itself between them, it grows ---- it
becomes a month, a year, a century; it becomes too
late.

Jean Giraudoux

Delicacy and Love

Love lessens woman's delicacy and increases man's.

Jean Paul Richter

Dependence and Love

It is sad my emotional dependence on the man I love should have killed so much of my energy and ability; there was certainly once a great deal of energy in me.

Sonya Tolstoy (wife of Leo Tolstoy)

It is easier to live through someone else than to become complete yourself.

Betty Friedan

Devotion and Love

Devotion is the exercise of love, by which it grows.

Robert Louis Stevenson

Direction of Love

Love does not consist in gazing at each other but in looking outward together in the same direction.

Antoine de Saint-Exupery
Wind, Sand, and Stars, 1939

Think not that you can direct the course of love, for love, if it finds you worthy, directs your course.

Kahlil Gibran
The Prophet, 1923

Divorce and Love

People wouldn't get divorced for such trivial reasons if they didn't get married for such trivial reasons.

Anonymous

Of course there is such a thing as love, or there wouldn't be so many divorces.

Ed Howe

I'm a wonderful housekeeper. Every time I get a divorce, I keep the house.

Zsa Zsa Gabor

If you made a list of the reasons why any couple got married, and another list of the reasons for their divorce, you'd have a hell of a lot of overlapping.

Mignon McLaughlin
The Neurotic's Notebook, 1963

Sometimes, if your own life is to add up, you must subtract yourself from someone else's life. This time comes, I think, whenever you find that the affection or love of someone else can be kept only at the cost of yourself. If you are on the receiving end of much criticism, if the other has nothing but dissatisfaction with you, if you have lost the sense that to be yourself is a good and decent thing, it is time to get out. If love lessens you, if an undeclared war is being carried on in its name, if it is an excuse for destructive demands, if it is painful and joyless, it is time to let the love go and save yourself. You will find another love but never another self.

Jo Coudert
Advice from a Failure, 1965

You never really know a man until you divorce him.

Zsa Zsa Gabor

Be careful whom you marry because divorce is forever.

Anonymous

Domination and Love

Love does not dominate; it cultivates.

Johann Wolfgang von Goethe

Men who say they are the boss in their own home will lie about other things, too.

Anonymous

Duty to Love

Only when it is a duty to love, only then is love eternally and happily secured against despair.

Soren Kierkegaard

Education and Love

The education of a woman's heart is a series of lessons with a series of men until she falls in love for the rest of her life.

Maurice Zolotow
Marilyn Monroe: A Biography, 1960

What is truly indispensable for the conduct of life has been taught by woman ---- the small rules of courtesy, the actions that win us the warmth or deference of others; the words that assure us welcome; the attitudes that must be varied to mesh with character or situations; all social strategy. It is listening to women that teaches us to speak to men.

Remy de Gourmont

Education is an admirable thing. But it is well to remember from time to time that nothing that is worth knowing can be taught.

Oscar Wilde

Elopement and Love

If it were not for the presents, an elopement would be preferable.

George Ade

Embarrassment and Love

We perceive when love begins and when it declines by our embarrassment when alone together.

Jean de La Bruyere
Characters, 1688

Would it embarrass you very much if I were to tell you. . . that I love you?

Anonymous

Emotional Acceptance and Love

Emotional acceptance is both the goal of love and the means toward the goal. The experience of love is created when our perception is not being distorted by me-vs.-them perceptions. Love is the experience of others as us, and not separately as him, her or them.

Ken Keyes, Jr.
A Conscious Person's Guide to Relationships, 1979

Emptiness and Love

Love and emptiness in us are like the sea's ebb and flow.

Kahlil Gibran

Enemies and Love

The Bible tells us to love our neighbors and also to love our enemies, probably because they are generally the same people.

G. K. Chesterton

Instead of loving your enemies, treat your friends a little better.

Anonymous

Energy and Love

Love is an energy which exists of itself. It is its own value.

Thornton Wilder

Love is an energy, an all-existing substance. It's noticed most when you don't have negative thoughts; then you notice love everywhere. If you have a lot of negative thoughts, you don't notice it. When you're feeling very positive, you feel love everywhere and you see it everywhere.

Sondra Ray

Essence of Love

Love consists in this: that two solitudes protect and touch and greet each other.

Rainer Maria Rilke
Letters to a Young Poet, 1904

Eternity and Love

He is not a lover who does not love forever.

Euripides

Love would be naught without the belief that it would last forever; love grows great through constancy.

Honore de Balzac
As quoted in *The Wisdom of Balzac,* 1923

Exaggeration and Love

Love is a gross exaggeration of the difference between one person and everyone else.

George Bernard Shaw

No woman ever falls in love with a man unless she has a better opinion of him than he deserves.

Ed Howe

A lover is a man who endeavors to be more amiable than it is possible for him to be; this is the reason why almost all lovers are ridiculous.

S.R.N. Chamfort
Maximes et Pensees, 1803

Existence and Love

If love is the answer, what is the question?

Uta West

Love is the only sane and satisfactory answer to the problems of human existence.

Erich Fromm
The Art of Loving, 1956

Expectations and Love

There is hardly any activity, any enterprise, which is started with such tremendous hopes and expectations, and yet which fails so regularly, as love.

Erich Fromm
The Art of Loving, 1956

We are ordinarily so indifferent to people that when we have invested one of them with the possibility of giving us joy, or suffering, it seems as if he must belong to some other universe, he is imbued with poetry.

Marcel Proust
Remembrance of Things Past, 1913-1927

It is astonishing how people persist in believing that if they could just have what they wanted, or at least what they think they want, then everything would be wonderful; they would have no further problems. "If I were just loved and cared for, I would be fine." In fact, most people today are much less prepared for being loved than they are for anger and disdain. We forget that the problem is in us, and we insist on seeing it in terms of those outside *ourselves*.

Thomas Patrick Malone and Patrick Thomas Malone
The Art of Intimacy, 1987

Nothing is as good as it seems beforehand.

George Eliot

Expression of Love

They love indeed who quake to say they love.

Philip Sidney
Astrophel and Stella, 1591

One expresses well only the love he does not feel.

Jean Baptiste Alphonso Karr

The Eye and Love

An eye can threaten like a loaded and leveled gun, or insult like hissing or kicking; or, in its altered mood, by beams of kindness, it can make the heart dance with joy.

Ralph Waldo Emerson

Tears are the noble language of the eyes.

Robert Herrick

Falling in Love

To fall in love is awfully simple, but to fall out of love is simply awful.

Anonymous

Many a man has fallen in love with a girl in a light so dim he would not have chosen a suit by it.

Maurice Chevalier

One does not fall "in" or "out" of love. One grows in love.

Leo Buscaglia
Love, 1972

Of all the misconceptions about love the most powerful and pervasive is the belief that "falling in love" is love or at least one of the manifestations of love. It is a potent misconception, because falling in love is subjectively experienced in a very powerful fashion as an experience of love. When a person falls in love, what he or she certainly feels is "I love him" or "I love her." But two problems are immediately apparent. The first is that the experience of falling in love is specifically a sex-linked erotic experience. We do not fall in love with our children even though we may love them very deeply. We do not fall in love with our friends of the same sex ---- unless we are homosexually oriented ---- even though we may care for them greatly. We fall in love only when we are consciously or unconsciously sexually motivated. The second problem is that the experience of falling in love is invariably temporary. No matter whom we fall in love with, we sooner or later fall out of love if the relationship continues long enough. This is not to say that we invariably cease loving the person with whom we fell in love. But it is to say that the feeling of ecstatic lovingness that characterizes the experience of falling in love always passes. The honeymoon always ends. The bloom of romance always fades. . . .

The essence of the phenomenon of falling in love is a sudden collapse of a section of an individual's boundaries, permitting one to merge his or her identity with that of another person. This sudden release of oneself from oneself, the explosive pouring out of oneself into the beloved, and the dramatic surcease of loneliness accompanying this collapse of ego boundaries is experienced by most of us as ecstatic. We and our beloved are one! Loneliness is no more!

M. Scott Peck
The Road Less Traveled, 1978

I have drunk the wine of life at last, I have known the best thing worth knowing, I have been warmed through, never to grow quite cold again till the end.

Edith Wharton
(on falling in love for the first time at age 46)

False Love

When you were a child, I crept into your dreams. Dazzlingly attractive, glamorous, and mysterious, I promised to make you happy forever after.

When you grew up, I kept beckoning, I would sweep you off your feet, make your pulse race and your spirits soar. I thrilled you with excitement, romance, and passion. I vowed the spell would never fade ---- and then I broke your heart. I AM FALSE LOVE.

Stan J. Katz and Aimee E. Liu
False Love and Other Romantic Illusions, 1988

Family and Love

For millions of men and women the family is the one and only setting in which human relationships are not governed predominantly by considerations of bargaining.

Mascall

Fantasy and Love

Love, such as it is in society, is only the exchange of two fantasies, and the contact of two bodies.

S. R. N. Chamfort
Maximes et Pensees, 1803

Fate and Love

Love is a flower, the seed of which is brought by the wind and blossoms where it drops. It is as ridiculous to be angry with a woman because she does not love us as to be angry with fate for not giving us black hair when we have red.

Honore de Balzac
As quoted in *The Wisdom of Balzac,* 1923

Faults and Love

A wife is to thank God her husband hath faults. A husband without faults is a dangerous observer.

Halifax

We may, if we choose, make the worst of one another. Everyone has his weak points; everyone has his faults; we may make the worst of these; we may fix attention constantly upon these. But we may also make the best of one another. We may put ourselves in the place of others, and ask what we should wish to be done to us, and thought of us, were we in their place. By loving whatever is lovable in

53

those around us, love will flow back from them to us, and life will become a pleasure instead of a pain; and earth will become like heaven; and we shall become not unworthy followers of Him whose name is Love.

Arthur Penrhyn Stanley

Faults are thick where love is thin.

James Howell

Fear and Love

No one loves the man whom he fears. There are only two emotions; one is Love and the other is Fear. Love is our true reality. . . . Fear always distorts our perception and confuses us as to what is going on. Love is the total absence of fear. Love asks no questions. Its natural state is one of extensions and expansion, not comparison and measurement. Love, then, is really everything that is of value, and fear can offer us nothing because it *is* nothing. . . . Fear is really a call for help, and therefore a request for Love.

Gerald G. Jampolsky
Love is Letting Go of Fear, 1979

First Love

The magic of first love is our ignorance that it can ever end.

Benjamin Disraeli

Every young girl tries to smother her first love in possessiveness. Oh what tears and rejection await the girl who imbues her first delicate match with fantasies of permanence, expecting that he at this gelatinous stage will fit with her in a finished puzzle for all the days.

Gail Sheehy

Men always want to be a woman's first love. That is their clumsy vanity. Women have a more subtle instinct about things: What they like is to be a man's last romance.

Oscar Wilde
A Woman of No Importance, 1894

Flowers and Love

When a man brings his wife flowers for no reason -- there's a reason.

Molly McGee

If one wants to see the manifestation of God's face on earth one merely has to look at, touch or smell a flower. And it should be remembered that any human being treated with kindness and love over a sufficiently long period will open up into an incredible flower not thought possible at the start.

Gil Friedman

Food and Love

Love and food are equally vital to our sanity and survival.

Kuo Tzu

Better a meal of vegetables where there is love than a fattened calf with hatred.

Proverbs 15:17 (NW)

Love is feeding everybody.

John Denver

Love, like man himself, dies of overeating more often than of hunger.

Jean Paul Richter

Love is the food of the universe. It is the most important ingredient in life. Children go towards love, they thrive on love and grow on love, and would die without it.

Sanaya Roman
Living with Joy, 1986

Never would it occur to a child that sheep, pigs, cows or chickens were good to eat, while, like Milton's *Adam,* he would readily make a meal of fruit, nuts, thyme, mint, peas and broad beans, which penetrate further and stimulate not only the appetite but other vague and deep nostalgias.

Cyril Connolly
The Unquiet Grave, 1945

Forgetfulness and Love

A woman is more responsive to a man's forgetfulness than to his attentions.

Jarson

Who loves well, forgets slowly.

French proverb

Forgiveness and Love

Love is an act of endless forgiveness, a tender look which becomes a habit.

Peter Ustinov

We can forgive as long as we love.

Francois de La Rochefoucauld
Maxims, 1665

Of him that hopes to be forgiven, it is indispensably required that he forgive. It is therefore superfluous to urge any other motive.

Samuel Johnson

To forgive is the highest,
Most beautiful form of love.
In return you will receive
Untold peace and happiness.

Robert Muller

Sometimes we find it hard to forgive. We forget that forgiveness is as much for us as for the other person. If you can't forgive it's like holding a hot coal in your hand ---- you're the one getting burned. The tension may be hurting you much more than the other person.

Jennifer James
Success is the Quality of Your Journey, 1983

Many people think forgiveness is only about other peoples' actions. Since most everyone is his or her own worst critic, learning to forgive oneself is where the real work on forgiveness must begin. Once we learn to forgive ourselves, learning to forgive others is "child's play."

Gil Friedman

Always forgive your enemies ---- nothing annoys them so much.

Oscar Wilde

Friendship and Love

Friend: One who knows all about you and loves you just the same.

Elbert Hubbard

Love is strongest in pursuit; friendship in possession.

Ralph Waldo Emerson

To live with someone and to live in someone are two fundamentally different matters. There are people in whom one can live without living with them, and vice versa. To combine both requires the purest degree of love and friendship.

Johann Wolfgang von Goethe

Each friend represents a world in us, a world possibly not born until they arrive, and it is only by this meeting that a new world is born.

Anais Nin

A girl happened to say to me that she "didn't sleep with her friends," and it struck me how odd a turn of phrase that was. One had to wonder if that meant that she considered the people with whom she did go to bed to be her enemies. Friends are the people who pick you up when someone knocks you down, and help you lick your wounds when love goes awry, so they are the ones who love you, not the other way around, and if you find that you are putting most of your energy into people who put you down rather than into those who build you up, it is certainly time to ask yourself who loves you and who does not.

Merle Shain
When Lovers Are Friends, 1978

We cherish our friends not for their ability to amuse us, but for ours to amuse them.

Evelyn Waugh

By friendship I mean, the greatest love and the greatest usefulness, and the most open communication, and the noblest sufferings, and the most exemplary faithfulness, and the severest truth, and the heartiest counsel, and the greatest union of mind, of which brave men and women are capable.

Jeremy Taylor

Sooner or later you've heard about all your best friends have to say. Then comes the tolerance of real love.

Anonymous

Physical attraction aside, lovers must be friends. If you and your partner get to know each other over a period of weeks or months before becoming romantically involved, you can develop trust and affection for each other as individuals without your vision being clouded by infatuation. Not only will this increase your chances of achieving true love, but it probably also will benefit your sexual relationship in the long run. From the start, your sex life will be enhanced by the tenderness and caring you've developed as friends. Furthermore, when you understand that physical attraction is just one of many bonds that hold you together, you can accept the highs and lows of sexual excitement as a normal part of true love.

Stan J. Katz and Aimee E. Liu
False Love and Other Romantic Illusions, 1988

Animals are such agreeable friends ---- they ask no questions, they pass no criticisms.

George Eliot

Friendship is a strong and habitual inclination in two persons to promote the good and happiness of each other.

Joseph Addison

A friend is another self.

Aristotle

Friendship renders prosperity more brilliant, while it lightens adversity by sharing and making its burden common.

Cicero

However rare true love is, true friendship is even rarer.

Francois de La Rochefoucauld
Maxims, 1665

A friend knows how to allow for mere quantity in your talk, and only replies to quality.

Anonymous

Wherever you are it is your friends that make your world.

William James

If I were to marry again tomorrow, I wouldn't give up one friend. I'd take them all with me as a sort of dowry and tell my new husband that he was getting a rich wife.

Merle Shain
When Lovers Are Friends, 1978

The friendships which last are those wherein each friend respects the other's dignity to the point of not really wanting anything from him. Therefore a man with a will to power can have no friends. He is like a boy with a chopper. He tries it on flowers, he tries it on sticks, he tries it on furniture, and at last he breaks it on a stone.

Cyril Connolly

One's friends are that part of the human race with which one can be human.

George Santayana

Constant use had not worn ragged the fabric of their friendship.

Dorothy Parker

Friendship is only purchased with friendship.

Anonymous

When a friend asks, there is no tomorrow.

Anonymous

There are no rules for friendship. It must be left to itself. We cannot force it any more than we can force love.

Anonymous

All relationships, whether they be romantic, business or fraternal, that are built on friendship have a solid foundation upon which to grow and prosper. Those relationships based on other factors, whether they be beauty, power, fame, fortune, or utility, are all destined to failure because their foundation is based on something that sooner or later will disappear. Therefore the main thing we must do in all our relationships is to establish, cultivate and maintain friendships. And the most important friendship to establish, cultivate and maintain is that of oneself.

Gil Friedman

The happiest moments of my life have been the flow of affection among friends.

Thomas Jefferson

I was extremely involved with love and romance when I was younger, and I rushed like a mad person trying to resolve my conflicts — but now I think the greatest thing that has happened to me is the wonderful friends I've made along the way. They are people I can really count on. This is the love that's really important. I had to be older, to have lived my life, to come to this truth. I was very involved with romantic love for years, but I don't think romantic relationships, as exciting as they are at first, last as we might wish. The great marriages, I believe, are those in which the partners become friends.

Liz Smith
As quoted by Walter Anderson in *The Greatest Risk of All,*
1988

A friend is a present you give yourself.

Robert Louis Stevenson

A faithful friend is the medicine of life.

Ecclesiastes 6:16

It takes practice to be a good friend, and we all make mistakes. Friendship, like love, is something you do, something you give that comes back to you.

Jennifer James
Success is the Quality of Your Journey, 1983

A friend may well be reckoned the masterpiece of nature.

Ralph Waldo Emerson

Friendship is unnecessary, like philosophy, like art . . . It has no survival value; rather it is one of those things that give value to survival.

C. S. Lewis

Frivolous Love

The ability to love frivolously is the chief characteristic which distinguishes human beings from beasts.

Heywood Campbell Broun

Genius and Love

Neither a lofty degree of intelligence nor imagination nor both together go to the making of genius. Love, love, love ---- that is the soul of genius.

Wolfgang Amadeus Mozart

Gifts and Love

Giving a gift is the most elegant way of expressing love.

Swami Chinmayaananda
Reflections, 1987

You can always try to teach people to love you in your style, but never expect anyone, no matter how close, to read your mind and heart. Tell them what you want. The investment you make in surprise is often a hidden expectation that brings disappointment.

Better yet, buy yourself your heart's desire. Don't turn special days into tests of love. Take care of yourself in the style you prefer ---- yours. Then, anything else you receive on that day will seem like extra love that you can enjoy without hurtful expectations.

Jennifer James
Success is the Quality of Your Journey, 1983

Giving Love

When we give from a place of love,
Rather than from a place of expectation,
More usually comes back to us
Than we could ever have imagined.

Susan Jeffers
Feel The Fear and Do It Anyway, 1987

Giving love to others is directly related to how much love you have for yourself.

Wayne W. Dyer
Your Erroneous Zones, 1976

Love wasn't put in your heart to stay,
Love isn't love till you give it away.

Anonymous

You can offer your love completely to hundreds of people and still retain the same love you had originally. It is like knowledge. The wise man can teach all he knows and when he's through he'll still know all that he has taught.

Leo Buscaglia
Love, 1972

While it is beautiful to give, you can create the feeling of separateness if your ego keeps pointing out what you have given. The consistent winners in the love game learn to love and serve others without the self-consciousness that they ---- as separate individuals ---- are doing it.

So, in choosing someone to live with, it may be wise to ask if you feel that the unfolding of your life is in harmony with sharing life's games in a way that will contribute to the well-being of your partner as s/he sees his or her well-being. This means looking deeply into your heart and mind to see to what extent you can appreciate your relationship as an opportunity to love and serve your beloved. And this means giving him or her what s/he wants ---- not what you think s/he should want. There's a lot of difference!

Ken Keyes, Jr.
A Conscious Person's Guide to Relationships, 1979

God and Love

The good news, which the World Redeemer brings and which so many have been glad to hear, zealous to preach, but reluctant, apparently, to demonstrate, is that God is love, that He can be, and is to be, loved, and that all without exception are His children.

Joseph Campbell
The Hero with a Thousand Faces, 1949

The heart of him who truly loves is a paradise on earth; he has God in himself, for God is love.

Robert de Lamennais

All love should be simply stepping-stones to the love of God. So it was for me; and blessed be His name for His great goodness and mercy.

Plato

To fall in love is to create a religion that has a fallible God.

Jorge Luis Borges
Other Inquisitions, 1958

With the love of God will come, as a sure effect, the love of everyone in the universe. The nearer we approach God, the more do we begin to see that all things are in Him. When the soul acquires the bliss of this supreme love, it also begins to see Him in everything. Our heart will thus become an eternal fountain of love.

Swami Vivekananda
Bhakti-Yoga

Grumbling and Love

Grumbling is the death of love.

Marlene Dietrich
Marlene Dietrich's ABC's, 1961

Half a Love

For all who move
In the mortal sun
Halfway warm
Is better than freezing
As half a love
Is better than none.

Phyllis McGinley
The Love Letters of Phyllis McGinley, 1954

Happiness and Love

Love is trembling happiness.

Kahlil Gibran
Spiritual Sayings of Kahlil Gibran, 1962

Love is the most terrible and also the most generous of the passions; it is the only one that includes in its dreams the happiness of someone else.

J. P. Kerr

To love is to place our happiness in the happiness of another.

Gottfried Wilhelm Leibnitz

Happiness is the secure feeling of being loved and needed by those I need and love.

Anonymous

It is well to remember that *none of us depends entirely on another for our happiness,* although we may think we do. It is not the person we love who is responsible for our depth of feeling. This feeling is part of ourselves, is our capacity to love, and it stays with us despite misfortune.

Claire Weekes
Hope and Help for Your Nerves, 1969

To bewail the loss of a person we love is a happiness compared with the necessity of living with one we hate.

Jean De La Bruyere
Characters, 1688

The most happy marriage I can picture. . . would be the union of a deaf man to a blind woman.

Samuel Taylor Coleridge

With love one can live even without happiness.

Fyodor Dostoevsky
Notes from the Underground, 1864

Perhaps the biggest source of unhappiness in the world today stems from the idea that there is someone out there who will meet all our needs, because it turns us into needful children, waiting to be fed, instead of healthy adults asking if there is anyone who might need us. We are not vessels in need of filling up, we are persons in our own right with resources of our own.

Merle Shain
When Lovers Are Friends, 1978

They grew to be so happy that even when they were two worn-out old people, they kept on. . . playing together like dogs.

Anonymous

The fountain of content must spring up in the mind, and he who has so little knowledge of human nature as to seek happiness by changing anything but his own disposition will waste his life in fruitless efforts and multiply the griefs he proposes to remove.

Samuel Johnson

If your whole happiness depends on one person then certainly you become a function of this person, which surely cannot be right.

Maurice Nicoll
Psychological Commentaries on the Teachings of Gurdjieff and Ouspensky, Volume 2 (1952)

Success is getting what you want. Happiness is wanting what you get

Anonymous

Most folks are about as happy as they make up their mind to be.

Abraham Lincoln

Hatred and Love

Hatred, like love, is fed on the merest trifles. Everything adds to it. Just as the one we love can do no wrong, the one we hate can do nothing right.

Honore de Balzac
As quoted in *The Wisdom of Balzac,* 1923

Love is nothing but joy accompanied with the idea of an external cause, and *hatred* is nothing but sorrow with the accompanying idea of an external cause.

Baruch Spinoza
Ethics, 1670

Healing and Love

There is a force, an energy that we can all evoke that profoundly facilitates the healing process. This energy is sufficient to stimulate the healing process naturally inherent in the physical form. This energy is love ---- a real energy that has physiologic impact and is transmittable.

Leonard Laskow

The fundamental problem most patients face is an inability to love themselves, having been unloved by others during some crucial part of their lives. This period is almost always childhood, when our relations with our parents establish our characteristic way of reacting to stress. As adults we repeat these reactions and make ourselves vulnerable to illness, and our personalities often determine the specific nature of the illness. The ability to love oneself, combined with the ability to love life, fully accepting that it won't last forever, enables one to improve the quality of life.

Bernie S. Siegel
Love, Medicine and Miracles, 1986

Health and Love

The true index of a man's character is the health of his wife.

Cyril Connolly
The Unquiet Grave, 1945

Nearly all destruction or self-destruction, almost all hatred and sorrow, almost all greed and possessiveness, spring from starvation of love and sex.

Jolan Chang
The Tao of Love and Sex, 1977

Under the sustaining influence of love, the physical body is always at its best. It is probably true that more people are sick from lack of love in their lives than from all other causes put together.

Eric Butterworth
Life is for Loving, 1973

Help and Love

Love is all we have, the only way that each can help the other.

Euripides

Home and Love

Grief, like pleasure, infects the atmosphere. A first glance into any home is enough to tell you whether love or despair reigns there.

Honore de Balzac
As quoted in *The Wisdom of Balzac,* 1923

Honeymoon and Love

The honeymoon is not actually over until we cease to stifle our sighs and begin to stifle our yawns.

Helen Rowland

The honeymoon is over when the dog brings your slippers and your wife barks at you.

Anonymous

Hope and Love

A very small degree of hope is sufficient to cause the birth of love.

Stendhal
On Love, 1822

The Human Psyche and Love

We study the human psyche through analysis; we heal it through love.

Sigmund Freud

Humor and Love

The man and woman who can laugh at their love, who can kiss with smiles and embrace with chuckles, will outlast in mutual affection all the throat-lumpy, cow-eyed couples of their acquaintance. Nothing lives on so fresh and evergreen as the love with a funnybone.

George Jean Nathan

Few men are much worth loving in whom there is not something well worth laughing at.

Anonymous

Among those whom I like or admire, I can find no common denominator, but among those whom I love, I can: all of them make me laugh.

W. H. Auden
The Dyer's Hand, 1962

A difference of taste in jokes is a great strain on the affections.

George Eliot
Daniel Deronda, 1876

Husbands and Love

To catch a husband is an art, to keep him, a job.

Simone de Beauvoir

Husbands are like fires; they go out when unattended.

Zsa Zsa Gabor

The majority of husbands remind me of an orangutan trying to play the violin.

Honore de Balzac
As quoted in *The Wisdom of Balzac,* 1923

It takes a smart husband to have the last word and not use it.

Anonymous

There is so little difference between husbands you might as well keep the first.

Adela Rogers St. John

A wife can be wonderful at accepting love initiated by the husband, amplifying it manyfold, and reflecting it to him and the children, filling the home with an inexplicably wonderful climate. But the husband must take the responsibility of initiating love. Husbands who have found this secret are to be envied. The love returned to him by his wife is price-less, in my opinion the most precious commodity in this world. It is difficult to initiate love at first, but as the husband experiences his wife's love in return, he finds it to be multiplied many times, and sees that as this love increases with time, it becomes easier and easier to do.

Ross Campbell
How to Really Love Your Child, 1978

Ideal Love

Ideal love is a lie put forth by poets.

Alphonse Daudet

Illusions and Love

Love is a child of illusion and the parent of disillusion.

Miguel de Unamuno
Tragic Sense of Life, 1921

It's love's illusions I recall
I really don't know love at all.

Joni Mitchell
Both Sides Now, 1967

Love has its illusions, and every illusion has its morrow.

Honore de Balzac
As quoted in *The Wisdom of Balzac,* 1923

Importance of Love

Love is more important than your precious image. Love is more important than money. Love is more important than rules. Love is more important than being right. Love is more important than efficiency. Love is more important than sleep. Love is more important than sex. Love is more important than being on time. Love is more important than getting your own way. Love is more important than the taste of food. Love is more important than people meeting your models. Love is more important than your plans. Love is more important than having time alone. Love is more important than your success. Love is more important than your health. Love is more important than your pride or prestige. Love is more important than having a skinny figure. **LOVE IS MORE IMPORTANT THAN ANYTHING ELSE!**

Ken Keyes, Jr.
How to Enjoy Your Life in Spite of It All, 1980

A thought transfixed me: for the first time in my life I saw the truth as it is set into song by poets, proclaimed as the final wisdom by so many thinkers. The truth ---- that love is the ultimate and highest goal to which man can aspire. Then I grasped the meaning of the greatest secret that human poetry and human thought and belief have to impart: *The salvation of man is through love and in love.*

Viktor E. Frankl
Man's Search for Meaning, 1959

It doesn't matter who you love or how you love, but that you love.

Rod McKuen

To cheat oneself out of love is the most terrible deception; it is an eternal loss for which there is no reparation, either in time or in eternity.

Soren Kierkegaard

Incapacity to Love

The only abnormality is the incapacity to love.

Anais Nin

People who are sensible about love are incapable of it.

Douglas Yates

We can never at any time absorb more love than we're ready for.

Mignon McLaughlin
The Neurotic's Notebook, 1963

Independence and Love

Love is generally confused with dependence; but in point of fact, you can love only in proportion to your capacity for independence.

Rollo May

Indifference and Love

The opposite of love is indifference.

Rollo May
Man's Search for Himself, 1953

Infatuation vs. Love

Infatuation is instant desire. It is one set of glands calling to another. Love is friendship that has caught fire. It takes root and grows ---- one day at a time.

Infatuation is marked by a feeling of insecurity. You are excited by a feeling of insecurity. You are excited and eager, but not genuinely happy. There are nagging doubts, unanswered questions, little bits and pieces about your beloved that you would as soon not examine too closely. It might spoil the dream.

Love is quiet understanding and the mature acceptance of imperfection. It is real. It gives you strength and grows beyond you, to bolster your beloved. You are warmed by his presence, even when he is away. Miles do not separate you. You want him nearer. But near or far, you know he is yours and you can wait.

Infatuation says, "We must get married right away. I can't risk losing him."

Love says, "Be patient. Don't panic. Plan your future with confidence."

Infatuation has an element of sexual excitement. If you are honest, you will admit it is difficult to be in one another's company unless you are sure it will end in intimacy. Love is the maturation of friendship. You must be friends before you can be lovers.

Infatuation lacks confidence. When he's away, you wonder if he's cheating. Sometimes you check.

Love means trust. You are calm, secure and unthreatened. He feels that trust, and it makes him even more trustworthy.

Infatuation might lead you to do things you'll regret later, but love never does.

Love is an upper. It makes you look up. It makes you think up. It makes you a better person than you were before.

Ann Landers

Influence of Love

We are shaped and fashioned by what we love.

Johann Wolfgang von Goethe

Love makes all hard hearts gentle.

Proverb

A man is not where he lives, but where he loves.

Latin proverb

Jealousy and Love

Lots of people know a good thing the minute the other fellow sees it first.

Job E. Hedges

Jealousy is no more than feeling alone against smiling enemies.

Elizabeth Bowen

Jealousy, the jaundice of the soul.

John Dryden

Always remember, Peggy, it's matrimonial suicide to be jealous when you have a really good reason.

Clare Boothe Luce

Jealousy takes away the freedom of both the one who is jealous and the one who is possessed. If you give yourself what you need ---- be it attention, love, or something else ---- then you will not experience jealousy. . . . Jealousy implies scarcity, that there is not enough. Freedom implies abundance, that there is enough.

Sanaya Roman
Living with Joy, 1986

Joy and Love

Grief can take care of itself, but to get the full value of a joy you must have somebody to divide it with.

Mark Twain

Judging Love

Judged by its consequences, love is more akin to hate than to affection.

Francois de La Rochefoucauld
Maxims, 1665

We should never judge those whom we love. The affection that is not blind is no affection at all.

Honore de Balzac
As quoted in *The Wisdom of Balzac,* 1923

Karma and Love

It is written in the code of love: He who strikes the blow is himself struck down.

Hadewijch of Antwerp

Kindness and Love

I would like to have engraved inside every wedding band, "Be kind to one another." This is the Golden Rule of marriage, and the secret of making love last through the years.

Randolph Ray
My Little Church Around the Corner, 1957

None is so near the gods as he who shows kindness.

Seneca

The best portion of a good man's life,
His little, nameless, unremembered acts
Of Kindness and Love.

William Wordsworth

Tenderness and kindness are not signs of weakness and despair, but manifestations of strength and resolution.

Kahlil Gibran
Spiritual Sayings of Kahlil Gibran, 1962

Kind words can be short and easy to speak, but their echoes are truly endless.

Mother Teresa

Kissing and Love

A kiss can be a comma, a question mark or an exclamation point. That's the basic spelling that every woman ought to know.

Mistinguett

The kiss originated when the first male reptile licked the first female reptile, implying in a subtle, complimentary way that she was as succulent as the small reptile he had for dinner the night before.

F. Scott Fitzgerald

Let him kiss me with the kisses of his mouth ---- for your love is more delightful than wine.

Song of Solomon 1:2 (NW)

91

The easiest thing about love is kissing and holding hands.

Anonymous

Knowing Your Lover

It doesn't much matter whom one marries, for one is sure to find out next morning it was someone else.

Rogers

A man knows his companion in a long journey and a little inn.

Thomas Fuller

You don't know a woman until you have had a letter from her.

Ada Leverson

A woman need know but one man well, in order to understand all men; whereas a man may know all women and understand not one of them.

Helen Rowland

Learning to Love

Your earliest notions of love came not only from your own relationship with your parents but also from your impressions of their marriage. Watching them, you learned how men and women should treat each other, the roles they should assume, the posturing that is permissible between the sexes, and how the sexuality plays out in a relationship.

Stan J. Katz and Aimee E. Liu
False Love and Other Romantic Illusions, 1988

The principle of love is dynamic. Certainly love can change the world and it can change you. But it can only do so if you take the principle into the laboratory and roll up your sleeves. You learn to speak by speaking. You learn to walk by walking. And you learn to love by loving. There is no other way.

Eric Butterworth
Life is for Loving, 1973

Learning to love one other person completely teaches you how to love all people. Learning to love all that is unlovable in your husband or wife, learning how to rise above pettiness, disagreements, judgments, and human preoccupations, establishes in you a love for all humanity.

Barry Vissell and Joyce Vissell
The Shared Heart, 1984

Life and Love

However mean your life is, meet it and live; do not shun it and call it hard names. It is not so bad as you are. It looks poorest when you are richest. The faultfinder will find faults even in Paradise. Love your life, poor as it is. You may perchance have pleasant, thrilling, glorious hours, even in a poorhouse.

Henry David Thoreau

The absolute value of love makes life worthwhile, and so Man's strange and difficult situation acceptable. Love cannot save life from death; but it can fulfill life's purpose.

Arnold J. Toynbee

A life without love, without the presence of the beloved, is nothing but a mere magic-lantern show. We draw out slide after slide, swiftly tiring of each, and pushing it back to make haste for the next.

Johann Wolfgang von Goethe
Elective Affinities, 1809

No man loves life like him who is growing old.

Sophocles

Life is a flower of which love is the honey.

Victor Hugo

What a wonderful life I've had! I only wish I'd realized it sooner.

Colette

The three stages of life are: youth, middle age, and "You look great!"

Anonymous

It is not true that life is one damn thing after another ---- it's one damn thing over and over.

Edna St. Vincent Millay

How ridiculous and what a stranger he is who is surprised at anything that happens in life.

Marcus Aurelius

Love is not enough. It must be the foundation, the cornerstone, but not the complete structure. It is much too pliable. Too yielding.

Bette Davis

Life is 10 percent what you make it and 90 percent how you take it.

Anonymous

There is a land of the living and a land of the dead. The bridge is love; the only truth, the only survival.

Thornton Wilder
The Bridge of San Luis Rey, 1927

Love doesn't make the world go 'round. Love is what makes the ride worthwhile.

Franklin P. Jones

Lingerie and Love

Brevity is the soul of lingerie.

Dorothy Parker

Loneliness and Love

Love is something far more than desire for sexual intercourse; it is the principal means of escape from the loneliness which afflicts most men and women throughout the greater part of their lives.

Bertrand Russell
Marriage and Morals, 1929

If you are afraid of loneliness, don't marry.

Anton Chekhov

The surest way to be alone is to get married.

Gloria Steinem

The cure for loneliness, strange as it may seem, is not in more active involvement in the world, but in seeking active unfoldment from within of our essential self which has been isolated. The lonely person needs to cultivate the art of creative solitude, to plumb the depths of his inmost self through meditation, to get away from people and relationships and become established in the root of the reality in God ---- in love. Loneliness is not a longing for people but for God. Thus, the answer is not in the bingo parlor or friendship club or in social busyness. It is in self-discovery and self-realization. It is in reflection upon God as love, knowing that you are "loved with an everlasting love," and that you are always *in* love. You can never be alone!

Eric Butterworth
Life is for Loving, 1973

What a lovely surprise to finally discover how unlonely being alone can be.

Anonymous

Looking for Love

Don't look for love; give love ---- and you will find love looking for you.

Beth Black

When I was a young man, I vowed never to marry until I found the ideal woman. Well, I found her ---- but alas, she was waiting for the ideal man.

Robert Schuman

Love Affairs and Love

A love affair is a grafting operation. "What has once been joined, never forgets." There is a moment when the graft takes; up to then is possible without difficulty the separation which afterwards comes only through breaking off a great hunk of oneself, the ingrown fiber of hours, days, years.

Cyril Connolly
The Unquiet Grave, 1945

A waning love affair welcomes an infidelity as a release from constancy.

Francois de La Rochefoucauld
Maxims, 1665

Love and Loving

Love cannot be commanded.

Latin Proverb

If there is anything better than to be loved, it is loving.

Anonymous

There is a single magic, a single power, a single salvation, and a single happiness, and that is called loving.

Hermann Hesse

They do not love that do not show their love.

William Shakespeare
The Two Gentlemen of Verona, 1554-1555

Loving sought is good, but given unsought is better.

William Shakespeare
Twelfth Night, 1599-1600

Do not arouse or awaken love until it so desires.

Song of Solomon 2:7 (NW)

Love at First Sight

The world's greatest time saver.

Anonymous

The only true love is love at first sight; second sight dispels it.

Israel Zangwill

Whoever loved that loved not at first sight?

Christopher Marlowe and George Chapman
Hero and Leander, 1598

Love at first sight is only realizing an imagination that has always haunted us; or meeting with a face, or figure, or cast of expression in perfection that we have seen and admired in a less degree or in less favorable circumstances a hundred times before.

William Hazlitt

Loving and Being Loved

In love, there is always one who kisses and one who offers the cheek.

French proverb

It is easy for them who have never been loved to sneer at love.

Welsh proverb

In the majority of couples, love consists of one party loving and the other allowing themselves to be loved.

Anonymous

It is easier to love people who hate us than those who love us more than we wish.

Francois de La Rochefoucauld
Maxims, 1665

There's never anything wrong in love, Clara, it just happens. In the end it may not matter very much exactly who it was with.

Graham Greene
The Honorary Consul, 1973

No one has ever loved anyone the way everyone wants to be loved.

Mignon McLaughlin
The Neurotic's Notebook, 1963

There is no greater invitation to love than loving first.

St. Augustine

For some mysterious reason we are deeply ashamed of our desire to love and be loved. This deep and resonating desire appears at the center of each one of us, yet even the use of the word "love" by ourselves or others can make us uneasy. That one word is unlike almost every other in its power to ignite emotion.

Joseph Simons and Jeanne Reidy
The Risk of Loving, 1968

They say if one understands himself, he understands all people. But I say to you, when one loves people, he learns something about himself.

Kahlil Gibran
Spiritual Sayings of Kahlil Gibran, 1962

No human being can ever have enough love, handclasps and physical contact too, or better still ever give enough.

Jolan Chang
The Tao of Love and Sex, 1977

Keep love in your heart. A life without it is like a sunless garden when the flowers are dead. The consciousness of loving and being loved brings a warmth and richness to life that nothing else can bring.

Oscar Wilde

Lubricant and Love

Love is something you use, not something you fall into. You use it as a lubricant through life.

Anonymous

Lust vs. Love

Lust is nature's device to secure the continuation of the species, usually dissipates rapidly, and connects us with all other animals. Love is nature's device to help those survive who are already here, usually grows slowly, and connects us with God.

Gil Friedman

Marriage and Love

Is not marriage an open question, when it is alleged, from the beginning of the world, that such as are in the institution want to get out; and such as are out want to get in?

Ralph Waldo Emerson

Marriage is Heaven and Hell.

German proverb

What we love about love is the fever, which marriage puts to bed and cures.

Mignon McLaughlin
The Neurotic's Notebook, 1963

Love comes after the wedding.

Laplander proverb

Marriages made in Heaven are not exported.

Samuel Hoffenstein
Poems in Praise of Practically Nothing, 1928

Love is an ideal thing, marriage a real thing; a confusion of the real with the ideal never goes unpunished.

Johann Wolfgang von Goethe

Marriage has many pains, but celibacy has no pleasures.

Samuel Johnson

Marriage is an edifice that must be rebuilt everyday.

Andre Maurois

Marriage is like Marxism: sounds good, but does not work.

Anonymous

A marriage is like a long trip in a tiny rowboat: if one passenger starts to rock the boat, the other has to steady it; otherwise they will go to the bottom together.

David Reuben

If you want to read a book about love and marriage ---- you've got to buy two separate books.

Alan King

By all means marry. If you get a good wife, you will become very happy; if you get a bad one, you will become a philosopher ---- and that is good for every man.

Socrates

One of the good things that come of a true marriage is, that there is one face in which changes come without your seeing them; or rather there is one face which you can still see the same, through all the shadows which have gathered upon it.

George MacDonald

Love, the quest;
Marriage, the conquest;
Divorce, the inquest.

Helen Rowland

One thing about being married ---- your mistakes never go unnoticed.

Bern Williams

His wife might not be a clever woman, but she was a cosy woman, and there was a lot to be said for cosiness in this very uncosy world.

J.B. Priestly

A man in love is incomplete until he is married. Then he is finished.

Zsa Zsa Gabor

Marriage is popular because it combines the maximum of temptation with the maximum of opportunity.

George Bernard Shaw
Man and Superman, 1903

A happy marriage is a long conversation that always seems too short.

Andre Maurois
I Remember, I Remember, 1942

I never married because there was no need. I have three pets at home which answer the same purpose as a husband. I have a dog which growls every morning, a parrot which swears all the afternoon and a cat that comes home late at night.

Marie Corelli

When a girl marries she exchanges the attention of many men for the inattention of one.

Helen Rowland

Marriage is like twirling a baton, turning handsprings, or eating with chopsticks. It looks easy till you try it.

Anonymous

Marriage is an arrangement like the block booking of motion pictures in which a number of less desirable features must be accepted in order to obtain one or two major attractions.

Helen P. St. Boulanger

After a few years of marriage, a man can look right at a woman without seeing her ---- and a woman can see right through a man without looking at him.

Helen Rowland

Marriage: a process of finding out what sort of guy your wife would have preferred.

Anonymous

Deceive not thyself by over-expecting happiness in the marriage state. . . . Marriage is not like the hill of Olympus, wholly clear, without clouds.

Thomas Fuller

Before marriage the three little words are, "I love you"; after marriage they are, "Let's eat out."

Anonymous

There's one consolation about matrimony. When you look around you can always see somebody who did worse.

Warren H. Goldsmith

Marriage is much more necessary to a man than to a woman; for he is much less able to supply himself with domestic comforts.

Samuel Johnson

The three stages of marriage are: big deal, ordeal and new deal.

Anonymous

Before marriage a man will lie awake all night thinking about something you said; after marriage he'll fall asleep before you finish saying it.

Helen Rowland

Marriage is tolerable enough in its way if you're easygoing and don't expect too much from it. But it doesn't bear thinking about.

George Bernard Shaw
Getting Married, 1911

Mother to daughter upon her upcoming marriage: "He'll make an excellent first husband."

Anonymous

A single man has not nearly the value he would have in a state of union. He is an incomplete animal. He resembles the odd half of a pair of scissors.

Benjamin Franklin

Marriage is often disappointing, to the woman because the man doesn't change, and to the man because the woman does.

Anonymous

Two young ladies were talking about love and marriage. "The man I marry," the first one said, "must be bright and colorful and entertaining. Yet when I'm in the mood for peace and quiet, I'll want him to remain silent. I want him to be up to the minute on sports and politics and the news of the day. And I will want him to stay home nights with me." Her friend thought for a minute and said, "You don't want a husband; you want a TV set."

In magazine *Good Reading for Everyone*

Where there's marriage without love, there will be love without marriage.

Benjamin Franklin

The most difficult years of marriage are those following the wedding.

Anonymous

Marriage is a lot like the army, everyone complains, but you'd be surprised at the large numbers that reenlist.

James Garner

The greatest charm of marriage, in fact that which renders it irresistible to those who have once tasted it, is the dialogue, the permanent conversation between two people which talks over everything and everyone till death breaks the record. It is this which, in the long run, makes a reciprocal equality more intoxicating than any form of servitude or domination.

Cyril Connolly
The Unquiet Grave, 1945

Marriage Proposals and Love

Hardly any woman reaches the age of 30 without having been asked to marry, at least twice ---- once by her father; once by her mother.

Anonymous

Today, he admits, he gave his sons just one piece of advice: "Never confuse *I love you* with *I want to marry you.*

Cleveland Amory

When Woodrow proposed to me I was so surprised I nearly fell out of bed.

The second Mrs. Woodrow Wilson

Meanings of Love

Love has various lodgings; the same word does not always signify the same thing.

Voltaire
Philosophical Dictionary, 1764

The word "love" bridges for us those chasms of momentary indifference and boredom which gape from time to time between even the most ardent lovers.

Aldous Huxley
The Olive Tree, 1937

I define love thus: the will to extend one's self for the purpose of nurturing one's own or another's spiritual growth.

M. Scott Peck
The Road Loss Traveled, 1978

Love is. . .the ability and willingness to allow those that you care for to be what they choose for themselves, without any insistence that they satisfy you.

Wayne W. Dyer
Your Erroneous Zones, 1976

The human soul possesses the germ of that indescribable something which poets and philosophers have endeavored to describe by words and poems for centuries.

That something is a charm which throws a spell around itself, and whosoever comes near it remains enchanted and spellbound. It sweetens the bitter experiences of life and makes one forget the drudgery of this world. Although it cannot be defined, still it has been called by various names in different countries. In the English language it is called "Love."

All human affection is but the manifestation of the wonderful power of that love. It is the one power that governs our lives and is inseparable from our being. We do not ask what love is; instinctively we understand its nature.

Swami Abhedananda
Human Affection and Divine Love

Meditation and Love

If love cannot help you into meditation, nothing will help you.

Bhagwan Shree Rajneesh

Men and Love

Nothing unites two men so much as a similarity of views in the matter of womankind.

Honore de Balzac
As quoted in *The Wisdom of Balzac,* 1923

Methods of Love

Love will find a way.

Anonymous

Man makes love by braggadocio. Woman makes love by listening ---- once a woman passes a certain point in intelligence, she finds it almost impossible to get a husband; she simply cannot go on listening without snickering.

H. L. Mencken

Man has his will, but woman has her way.

Oliver Wendell Holmes, Sr.

Middle Age and Love

Middle age is when your back goes out more than you do.

Anonymous

Miracle of Love

This is the miracle that happens every time to those who really love: the more they give, the more they possess of that precious nourishing love from which flowers and children have their strength and which could help all human beings if they would take it without doubting. . . .

Rainer Maria Rilke

Mistress and Love

A man and his mistress are not bored when they are together because they are continually talking of themselves.

Francois de La Rochefoucauld
Maxims, 1665

Money and Love

Love is an ocean of emotions, entirely surrounded by expenses.

Thomas Robert Dewar

Don't marry for money; you can borrow it cheaper.

Scottish proverb

A fool and his money are soon married.

Carolyn Wells

The real paradox is that men who make, materially, the biggest sacrifices for their women should do the least for them ideally and romantically.

Edith Wharton

In Biblical times, a man could have as many wives as he could afford. Just like today.

Abigail Van Buren

We should always keep a little money in reserve for a time when it might be needed. This does not apply to love.

Bern Williams

A great love is a credit account open to such voracious drafts on it that the moment of bankruptcy is inevitable.

Honore de Balzac
As quoted in *The Wisdom of Balzac,* 1923

Love, like money, is offered most freely to those in least need of it.

Mignon McLaughlin
The Neurotic's Notebook, 1963

Who, being loved is poor?

Oscar Wilde
A Woman of No Importance, 1894

Motherly Love

The greatest love is a mother's; then comes a dog's; then comes a sweetheart's.

Polish proverb

Erotic love begins with separateness, and ends in oneness. Motherly love begins with oneness and ends in separateness.

Erich Fromm
The Sane Society, 1959

A mother's love does not have 20/20 vision.

Bern Williams

Mushrooms and Love

Love is like a mushroom. You never know whether it's the real thing until it's too late.

Anonymous

Mutual Love

To love one who also loves you, to admire one who admires you, in a word, to be the idol of one's idol is exceeding the limit of human joy, it is stealing fire from heaven.

Madame de Gerardio

There is nothing nobler or more admirable than when two people who see eye to eye keep house as man and wife, confounding their enemies and delighting their friends.

Homer
Odyssey, 9th century, BC

Mutual love, the crown of bliss.

John Milton

Mystery and Love

Love is like quicksilver in the hand. Leave the fingers open and it stays in the palm; clutch it and it darts away.

Dorothy Parker

Love is an endless mystery,
for it has nothing else to explain it.

> Rabindranath Tagore
> *Fireflies,* 1928

A woman is like your shadow; follow her, she flies; fly from her, she follows.

> S.R.N. Chamfort
> *Maximes et Pensees,* 1803

The men that women marry,
And why they marry them, will always be
A marvel and a mystery to the world.

> Henry Wadsworth Longfellow
> *Michael Angelo,* 1883

Mystery and disappointment are not absolutely indispensable to the growth of love, but they are often very powerful auxiliaries.

> Charles Dickens
> *Life and Adventures of Nicholas Nickleby,* 1839

To judge of a certain woman by her beauty, her youth, her pride, and her haughtiness, we would say that none but a hero would one day win her. But her choice is made: she loves a little monster with no brains.

> Jean de La Bruyere
> *Characters,* 1688

Need and Love

It is a beautiful necessity of our nature to love something.

Douglas William Jerrold

We want and really need someone who will be involved in our life. When we open that hidden part of ourselves even for a moment, we need someone who will react with us. We need someone who will share our strong emotions. We need someone so involved that he will be afraid with us, be glad with us, be depressed with us; who will expose his own humanity as we expose ours. It is this contact between two human beings, revealing their common sensitivities, which draws them from loneliness and joins them together.

Joseph Simons and Jeanne Reidy
The Risk of Loving, 1968

It is when we earn love least, that we need it most.

Anonymous

Neighborly Love

Love thy neighbor as thyself, but choose your neighborhood.

Louise Beal

Pain and Love

Pleasure of love lasts but a moment,
Pain of love lasts a lifetime.

Jean Pierre

One word frees us of all the weight and pain of life; that word is love.

Sophocles

Love anything that lives ---- a person, a pet, a plant ---- and it will die. Trust anybody and you may be hurt; depend on anyone and that one may let you down. The price of cathexis is pain. If someone is determined not to risk pain, then such a person must do without many things: having children, getting married, the ecstasy of sex, the hope of ambition, friendship ---- all that makes life alive, meaningful and significant. Move out or grow in any dimension and pain as well as joy will be your reward. A full life will be full of pain. But the only alternative is not to live fully or not to live at all.

M. Scott Peck
The Road Loss Traveled, 1978

Parenting and Love

You must love your children as well as parent them; simply parenting them is not enough. Parenting them prepares them to live in the world; loving them enables them to prosper emotionally in relationship and to find a quiet and beautiful delight in simply being, even when they are alone. We parent when we teach; we love when the sight of our children makes our hearts glad simply because they exist.

Thomas Patrick Malone and Patrick Thomas Malone
The Art of Intimacy, 1987

There is no question but that your parents failed you as parents. All parents fail their children, and yours are no exception. No parent is ever adequate for the job of being a parent, and there is no way not to fail at it. No parent ever has enough love, enough wisdom, or maturity, or whatever; no parent ever succeeds. This means that part of your task, like every other person, is to supplement what your parents have given you ---- to find other sources of parenting. You need more mothering than your mother could give you, more fathering than your father had to offer, more brothering and sistering than you got from your siblings.

The problems are complicated by the demands our society makes on parents to be good parents. They are supposed to be 100 percent adequate and it is a terrible disgrace if they are not. If they are successful their children will reward them with devoted love, obedience and success; if they are not, their children will turn out to be unloving, disobedient and unsuccessful. This is the prevailing conviction of our society. But when parents buy this notion they put themselves in an impossible position. They try first to be 100 percent adequate. When they inevitably fail at that, they try to "appear to be" 100 percent adequate. In either case they cling to you, demanding that you get all your parenting from them and thus reassure them that they have been good parents. Such parental concern about children's failures can be understood in part as an attempt to force the children to succeed and thus reassure the parents that they have been good parents.

They thus find it difficult to let you grow up ---- that is, to find other sources of parenting. This means that you will have to grow up in spite of them rather than wait for their permission. They will not make it easy for you and you must do it on your own.

To grow up it is necessary for you to forgive your parents, but you must forgive them for your sake, not theirs. Their self-forgiveness is up to them, not to you, and they cannot wait for you to forgive them any more than you can afford to wait for them to forgive you. When you do not forgive them it means that you are still expecting all your parenting from them. You are clinging to them in the hope that if you can make them feel guilty enough, they will finally come through with enough parenting, but this is impossible and in order for you to be really free to find other parenting, you must forgive.

I hope that you will not be embarrassed at your need for parenting, and that you will be humble enough and determined enough to find effective ways of getting it.

Henry T. Close
Voices: The Art and Science of Psychotherapy, Spring 1968

Passion and Love

The duration of passion is proportionate with the original resistance of the woman.

Honore de Balzac
As quoted in *The Wisdom of Balzac,* 1923

The same wind snuffs candles yet kindles fires; so, where absence kills a little love, it fans a great one.

Francois de La Rochefoucauld
Maxims, 1665

Our passions are like convulsive fits, which, though they make us stronger for the time, leave us weak ever after.

Jonathan Swift

Passionate love is a quenchless thirst.

Kahlil Gibran
Spiritual Sayings of Kahlil Gibran, 1962

Let men tremble to win the hand of woman, unless they win along with it the utmost passion of her heart.

Nathaniel Hawthorne

There is no arguing with passion. The slaves of their passions are as deaf as they are blind.

Honore de Balzac
As quoted in *The Wisdom of Balzac,* 1923

Every passion makes us commit faults, but love leads us into the most ridiculous blunders.

Francois de La Rochefoucauld
Maxims, 1665

Patience and Love

Patience is passion tamed.

Lyman Abbott

It takes patience to appreciate domestic bliss; volatile spirits prefer unhappiness.

George Santayana

Patience is bitter, but its fruit is sweet

Jean-Jacques Rousseau

A gift God gives only to those He loves.

Moroccan proverb

The biggest pitfall as you make your way through life is impatience. Remember that being impatient is simply a way of punishing yourself. It creates stress, dissatisfaction and fear. . . . Patience means knowing it will happen. . . and giving it time to happen.

Susan Jeffers
Feel The Fear And Do It Anyway, 1987

He who knows how to wait for what he desires does not feel very desperate if he fails in obtaining it; and he, on the contrary, who is very impatient in procuring a certain thing, takes so much pains about it that, even when he is successful, he does not think himself sufficiently rewarded.

Jean de La Bruyere
Characters, 1688

Peace and Love

In the presence of the loved one we rest in a serenity which permits the best expression of ourselves. There is not even a thought of doing or saying anything just to please the other. We know that whatever we spontaneously are will be enjoyed and appreciated simply because it is an expression of our own uniqueness. In place of our furtive search for the acceptable phrase or look we experience a calm which permits us to move into our real self and to discover its riches. . . .

For the atmosphere to be truly peaceful we ourselves need to have a sincere desire to experience the presence of the loved one. But we must desire to experience, not some ideal person we want the other to be but rather the other as he really is. By leaving aside our distorting ideal we are free to see in each word, look and gesture more of the person's basic reality. The calm can permit us to shed the goals we have for others and to begin discovering the complex mystery present before us.

Joseph Simons and Jeanne Reidy
The Risk of Loving, 1968

Perfect Love

Perfect love sometimes does not come till the first grandchild.

Welsh proverb

Pleasure and Love

The greatest pleasure of life is love.

William Temple

There is more pleasure in loving than in being loved.

Thomas Fuller
Gnomologia, 1732

The biggest difference of all differences in this world is between the ones that had or have pleasure in love and those that haven't and hadn't any pleasure in love, but just watched with sick envy.

Tennessee Williams
Sweet Bird of Youth, 1959

Whenever you are sincerely pleased you are nourished.

Ralph Waldo Emerson

Poetry and Love

I hope that one to two immortal lyrics will come out of all this tumbling about.

Louise Bogen
(of her affair with fellow poet Theodore Roethke)

Possessions and Love

Everything belonging to a loved one is precious.

P. A. C. de Beaumarchais
Le Marriage de Figaro, 1786

The most precious possession that ever comes to a man in this world is a woman's heart.

Holland

You are so naive, and do not understand that the love of possessions is but a shallow love, a tenuous joy that will not last. You have set your heart upon the acquisition of external things. From this comes misery and suffering! . . . What you call happiness is but a will o' the wisp, an illusion, which at any moment turns into greater misery than you have ever imagined. What has been given to you can be taken from you.

Buddha
As quoted by George N. Marshall in
Buddha, The Quest for Serenity, A Biography, 1978

Possessiveness and Love

Whatever quality we spontaneously prize in the other fascinates and delights us. It is as if we could never have enough contact with the quality we see as a natural element in the personality of the other. . . . Sooner or later the burden grows too heavy. Embarrassed and bewildered, the other person starts refusing some of our requests to see him. Irritation creeps into the relationship. Focusing so much on our own needs, we may never realize that we are the source of the trouble. In time, however, it becomes obvious that we are damaging the relationship we prize so dearly.

Joseph Simons and Jeanne Reidy
The Risk of Loving, 1973

Proper Motions and Love

If you go through the proper motions, you'll soon begin to feel the corresponding emotions.

George W. Grace

Proximity and Love

How distant I am from the people when I am with them, and how close when they are far away.

Kahlil Gibran
Spiritual Sayings of Kahlil Gibran, 1962

To be in the company of those whom we love satisfies us; it does not matter whether we dream of them, speak or not speak of them, think of them or think of indifferent things, as long as we are near them.

Jean de La Bruyere
Characters, 1688

Punishment and Love

Love is a spaniel that prefers even punishment from one hand to caresses from another.

Colton

Puppy Love

Puppy love: the beginning of a dog's life.

Anonymous

Pure Love

Pure love is matchless in majesty; it has no parallel in power and there is no darkness it cannot dispel.

Meher Baba

Reason and Love

Love is not ruled by reason.

Moliere
Le Misanthrope, 1666

The heart has reasons that reason does not understand.

Jacques Bossuet

To live is to love ---- all reason is against it, and all healthy instincts for it.

Samuel Butler

People who are not in love fail to understand how an intelligent man can suffer because of a very ordinary woman. This is like being surprised that anyone should be stricken with cholera because of a creature so insignificant as the common bacillus.

Marcel Proust
Remembrance of Things Past, 1913-1927

Men are like that ---- they can resist sound argument and yield to a glance.

Honore de Balzac
As quoted in *The Wisdom of Balzac,* 1923

Reflection and Love

You cannot love or hate something about another person unless it reflects something you love or hate about yourself.

Anonymous

My true relationship is my relationship with myself ---- all others are simply mirrors of it. As I learn to love myself, I automatically receive the love and appreciation from others that I desire. If I am committed to myself and to the truth, I will attract others with equal commitment. My willingness to be intimate with my own deep feelings creates the space for intimacy with another. Enjoying my own company allows me to have fun with whomever I'm with.

Shakti Gawain
Living in the Light, 1986

Relatives and Love

It is a mistake to suppose that relations must of course love each other because they are relations. Love must be cultivated, and can be increased by judicious culture, as wild-fruit may double their bearing under the hand of a gardener; and love can dwindle and die out by neglect, as choice flowerseeds planted in poor soil dwindle and grow single.

Harriet Beecher Stowe

In times of great stress, such as a four-day vacation, the thin veneer of family life wears off almost at once, and we are revealed in our true personalities.

Shirley Jackson

A man is reputed to have thought and elegance; he cannot, for all that, say a word to his cousin or uncle.

Ralph Waldo Emerson

Remedy for Love

There is no remedy for love but to love more.

Henry David Thoreau

There are various cures for love, but none is infallible.

Francois de La Rochefoucauld
Maxims, 1665

Respect and Love

Where we do not respect, we cease to love.

Benjamin Disraeli

Men who cherish for women the highest respect are seldom popular with them.

Joseph Addison

Revealing and Feigning Love

No disguise can mask love, nor feign it for long.

Francois de La Rochefoucauld
Maxims, 1665

Revolution and Love

Love is always revolutionary.

Andrei Voznesensky

Let me say. . . that the revolutionary is guided by a great feeling of love.

Che Guevara

Man must evolve for all human conflict a method which rejects revenge, aggression and re-taliation. The foundation of such a method is love.

Martin Luther King, Jr.

Reward of Love

Love is love's reward.

John Dryden

Risk and Love

The person who risks nothing, does nothing, has nothing, is nothing, becomes nothing. He may avoid suffering and sorrow, but he simply cannot learn and feel and change and grow and love and live. He has forfeited his freedom. Only the person who risks is truly free.

Anonymous

Romantic Love

Love is an infusion of intense feeling, a fine madness that makes you drunk, and when one is in love, life can be a succession of free falls while working without a net. Love permits the lover to savor rare emotions and dangerous sensations, and because one is never so alive as when one is in love, and never so full of power, there are people hooked on love who wouldn't consider taking drugs.

Merle Shain
Some Men Are More Perfect Than Others, 1973

In real love you want the other person's good. In romantic love you want the other person.

Margaret Anderson

Romance is the glamour which turns the dust of everyday life into a golden haze.

Elinor Glyn

Romantic love is the single greatest energy system in the Western psyche. In our culture it has supplanted religion as the arena in which men and women see meaning, transcendence, wholeness, and ecstasy. . . .

The reality that hides in romantic love is the fact of spiritual aspiration; the truth that the Western man unconsciously and involuntarily seeks in romantic love is the inner truth of his own soul. The Western man, without realizing it, is caught in a quest for wholeness and, against his wish, is pulled inexorably by a vision of the universal and the eternal. But it is in the image of woman, seen through the lens of romantic love, that he invests his quest and his vision. . . .

One of the great paradoxes in romantic love is that *it never produces human relationship* as *long* as *it stays romantic.* It produces drama, daring adventures, wondrous, intense love scenes, jealousies, and betrayal; but people never seem to settle into relationship with each other as flesh-and-blood human beings until they are out of the romantic love stage, until they *love* each other instead of being "in love."

In romantic love there is no friendship. Romance and friendship are utterly opposed energies, natural enemies with completely opposing motives. Sometimes people say, "I don't want to be friends with my husband [or wife]; it would take all the romance out of our marriage." It is true: Friendship does take the artificial drama and intensity out of a relationship, but it also takes away the egocentricity and the impossibility and replaces the drama with something human and real.

Robert A. Johnson
We: Understanding the Psychology of Romantic Love, 1983

142

Roots of Love

No one can say
Where love will take root.

> Barbara Howes
> *Indian Summer*

Sacrifice and Love

Love, whether sexual, parental, or fraternal, is essentially sacrificial, and prompts a man to give his life for his friends.

> George Santayana
> *The Life of Reason: Reason in Society,* 1905-1906

If you begin by sacrificing yourself to those you love, you will end by hating those to whom you have sacrificed yourself.

> George Bernard Shaw
> *Man and Superman,* 1903

Love is always expressed by making a sacrifice.

> Swami Chinmayaananda
> *Reflections,* 1987

Satisfaction and Love

If anyone is to remain pleased with you, he should be pleased with himself whenever he thinks of you.

Bradly

Second Love

A gentleman who had been very unhappy in marriage, married immediately after his wife died: Johnson said it was the triumph of hope over experience.

James Boswell
Life of Samuel Johnson, 1770

If the second marriage is a success, the first one really isn't a failure.

Mignon McLaughlin
The Neurotic's Notebook, 1963

Secret Love

There is a name hidden in the shadow of my soul, where I read it night and day and no other eyes have seen it.

Alphonse de Lamartine

As soon as you cannot keep anything from a woman, you love her.

Paul Geraldy

Seduction and Love

All really great lovers are articulate, and verbal seduction is the surest road to actual seduction.

David Mannes

Self-esteem and Love

Whenever someone is deprived of his self-esteem, he is deprived of the only thing that makes him a person worth loving. For one's own benefit, if for no other reason, the effort should be to build self-esteem in the other, to confirm rather than to assault it. This is achieved, not by flattery, but by a generous appreciation of the other's strengths and a generous deemphasis of his weaknesses, by speaking to his good points and as rarely as possible about his bad ones. People who are good to each other make each other good.

Jo Coudert
Advice from a Failure, 1965

Self-improvement and Love

I love you,
Not only for what you are,
But for what I am
When I am with you.
I love you,
Not only for what
You have made of yourself
But for what you are making of me.

Roy Crots

Self-love

I continue to explain that no matter what their problem seems to be, there is only one thing I ever work on with anyone, and this is *Loving the Self.* Love is the miracle cure. Loving ourselves works miracles in our lives.

I am not talking about vanity or arrogance or being stuck-up, for that is not love. It is only fear. I am talking about having a great respect for ourselves and a gratitude for the miracle of our body and our mind.

Louise L. Hay
You Can Heal Your Life, 1984

When you love yourself, you are secure and "within-dependent." You can face the changes in the world without threat. If you do not love yourself, you are not centered in the reality of yourself which is love. You are not letting yourself BE love. You are dependent for security on whether some other persons act lovingly toward you. In this consciousness every change in people and every changing condition is a threat that triggers in you a reaction of hate or resistance.

Eric Butterworth
Life is for Loving, 1973

To love oneself is the beginning of a lifelong romance.

Oscar Wilde

The quality of humor is perhaps one of the greatest doorways to self-love. The ability to laugh, to smile at others, and to put your problems into perspective is an evolved skill. Those who come from a high level of self-love are often humorous, have a great wit, and love to bring out the childlike playfulness in others. They are willing to be spontaneous, often find reasons to smile, are able to make others feel at ease and be happy themselves.

Sanaya Roman
Living with Joy, 1986

The problem is not to change the self. It is exactly opposite; it is somehow to contrive to abandon all efforts at changing the self.

Jo Coudert
Advice from a Failure, 1965

But if a man happens to find himself he has a mansion which he can inhabit with dignity all the days of his life.

James Michener

Service and Love

Love leads to service and service leads to peace.

Mother Teresa

Make your service of love a beautiful thing; want nothing else, fear nothing else and let love be free to become what love truly is.

Hadewijch of Antwerp

The object of love is to serve, not to win.

Woodrow Wilson

So long as we love, we serve; so long as we are loved by others, I would almost say that we are indispensable; and no man is useless while he has a friend.

Robert Louis Stevenson

Sex and Love

Sexuality throws no light upon love, but only through love can we learn to understand sexuality.

Eugen Rosenstock-Huessy

It is as absurd to say that a man can't love one woman all the time as it is to say that a violinist needs several violins to play the same piece of music.

Honore de Balzac
As quoted in *The Wisdom of Balzac,* 1923

Love is its own aphrodisiac and is the main ingredient for lasting sex.

Mort Katz

Sex: The pleasure is momentary; the expense is exorbitant; the position ridiculous.

G. K. Chesterton

Sex appeal is 50 percent what you've got and 50 percent what people think you've got.

Sophia Loren

There is need for variety in sex, but not in love.

Theodor Reik
Of Love and Lust, 1957

So long as the emotional feelings between the couple are right, so long as there is mutual trust and love, their bodies will invariably make the appropriate responses.

David M. Mace

I know nothing about sex because I was always married.

Zsa Zsa Gabor

You mustn't force sex to do the work of love or love to do the work of sex.

Mary McCarthy

Love is the answer; but while you are waiting for the answer, sex raises some pretty interesting questions.

Woody Allen

One thing I've learned in all these years is not to make love when you really don't feel it; there's probably nothing worse you can do to yourself than that.

Norman Mailer

Acting is not very hard. The most important things are to be able to laugh and cry. If I have to cry, I think of my sex life. And if I have to laugh, well, I think of my sex life.

Glenda Jackson

Orgasms really have very little to do with making love, and men who require their women to respond with a *petit mal* seizure that can be picked up on the Richter scale are not making love but asking for reassurance.

Merle Shain
Some Men Are More Perfect Than Others, 1973

The big difference between sex for money and sex for free is that sex for money usually costs a lot less.

Brendan Francis

During a memorable period, when we were both visiting a dental hospital for gum treatment, the nightly flossing, single-head and double-head brushing, plaque disclosing and mouth washing took so long it became a whole new form of contraception.

Maureen Lipman
How Was it for You? 1985

Civilized people cannot fully satisfy their sexual instinct without love.

Bertrand Russell
Marriage and Morals, 1929

Give me chastity and continence, but not just now.

St. Augustine

They made love as though they were an endangered species.

Peter DeVries

Women complain about sex more than men. Their gripes fall into two major categories: (1) Not enough. (2) Too much.

Ann Landers

If you put a nickel in a jar every time you make love during the first year of your relationship and then afterwards take a nickel out every time you make love, the chances are you will never get all your nickels out.

Anonymous

Shyness and Love

The other thing that represses the utterances of love is the characteristic *shyness* of the Anglo-Saxon blood. Oddly enough, a race born of two demonstrative, outspoken nations ---- the Germans and the

French ---- has an habitual reserve which is like neither. There is a powerlessness of utterance in our blood that we should fight against, and struggle outward towards expression. We can educate ourselves to it, if we know and feel the necessity; we can make it a Christian duty, not only to love, but to be loving ---- not only to be true friends, but to *show* ourselves friendly. We can make ourselves say the kind things that rise in our hearts and tremble on our lips ---- do the gentle and helpful deeds which we long to do and shrink back from; and, little by little, it will grow easier ---- the love spoken will bring back the answer of love ---- the kind deed will bring back a kind deed in return.

Harriet Beecher Stowe

Simplicity and Love

In order to love simply, it is necessary to know how to show love.

Fyodor Dostoevsky

Sin and Love

Hate the sin and love the sinner.

Mohandas Gandhi

Where there is love there is no sin.

Montenegrin proverb

Solitude and Love

But let there be spaces in your togetherness,
And let the winds of the heavens dance between you.
Love one another, but make not a bond of love:
Let it rather be a moving sea between the shores of
your souls.

Kahlil Gibran
The Prophet, 1923

A good marriage is that in which each appoints
the other guardian of his solitude.

Rainer Maria Rilke
Letters, 1892-1910; 1910-1926

Source of Love

Love cannot be born of mere determination, for through the exercise of will one can at best be dutiful. One may through struggle and effort succeed in bringing his external actions into conformity with his conception of what is right, but such action is spiritually barren, without the inward beauty of love. Love has to spring spontaneously from within; it is in no way amenable to any form of inner or outer force. Love and coercion can never go together; but though love cannot be forced on anyone, it can be awakened through love itself. Love is essentially self-communicative; those who do not have it catch it from those who have it. Those who receive love from others cannot be its recipients without giving a response which, in itself, is of the nature of love. True love is unconquerable and irresistible and goes on gathering power and spreading itself, until eventually it transforms everyone whom it touches. Humanity will attain to a new mode of being through the free and unhampered interplay of pure love from heart to heart.

Meher Baba
God to Man and Man to God, 1975

Spirituality and Love

Your mind will naturally seek the easiest person to be with, one with whom there is no struggle, no rough edges to work out, one with whom it is easy and comfortable. But your heart, your true inner self, will seek the person who can best help you in your search for truth. *The mind seeks an easy relationship. The heart seeks a spiritual partner.*

> Barry Vissell and Joyce Vissell
> *The Shared Heart,* 1984

Strength and Love

One cannot be strong without love. For love is not an irrelevant emotion; it is the blood of life, the power of reunion with the separated.

> Paul Tillich
> *The Eternal Now,* 19?3

Love is one of the most powerful energies of the universe. It is thousands of times stronger than anger, resentment or fear.

> Sanaya Roman
> *Living with Joy,* 1986

Success in Love

If you would marry wisely marry your equal.

Ovid

Success in love consists not so much in marrying the one person who can make you happy, as in escaping the many who could make you miserable.

Anonymous

Success in marriage is much more than finding the right person; it is a matter of being the right person.

Barnett Robert Brickner

Only choose in marriage a woman whom you would choose for a friend if she were a man.

Joseph Joubert

Keep your eyes wide open before marriage and half-shut afterwards.

Benjamin Franklin

A successful relationship is one in which two persons learn to get along happily without the things they have no right to expect anyway.

Anonymous

All married couples should learn the art of battle as they should learn the art of making love. Good battle is objective and honest —— never vicious or cruel. Good battle is healthy and constructive, and brings to a marriage the principle of equal partnership.

Ann Landers

Never take anything for granted.

Benjamin Disraeli

What is important to a relationship is a harmony of emotional roles and not too great a disparity in the general level of intelligence.

Anonymous

For a successful relationship, similar worldviews help. If a vegetarian is living with someone who doesn't believe a meal is a "meal" unless a piece of red meat sits in the center of the plate, every meal will be a potential battleground in an endless war.

Gil Friedman

The art of being wise is the art of knowing what to overlook.

William James

The great secret of successful marriage is to treat all disasters as incidents and none of the incidents as disasters.

Harold Nicholson

Never go to bed mad. Stay up and fight.

Phyllis Diller
Phyllis Diller's Housekeeping Hints, 1966

Often the difference between a successful marriage and a mediocre one consists of leaving about three or four things a day unsaid.

Harlan Miller

In a constructive marriage. . . the partners must regularly, routinely and predictably, attend to each other and their relationship no matter how they feel. . . . Couples sooner or later always fall out of love, and it is at the moment when the mating instinct has run its course that the opportunity for genuine love begins. It is when the spouses no longer feel like being in each other's company always, when they would rather be elsewhere some of the time, that their love begins to be tested and will be found to be present or absent

M. Scott Peck
The Road Less Traveled, 1978

When marrying, one should ask one's self this question: Do you believe that you will be able to converse well with the woman into your old age?

Friedrich Wilhelm Nietzsche
"All Too Human," 1878, in *The Portable Nietzsche,* 1978

Suffering and Love

Love does not cause suffering: what causes it is the sense of ownership, which is love's opposite.

Antoine de Saint-Exupery
The Wisdom of the Sands, 1948

We are healed of a suffering by experiencing it to the full.

Marcel Proust
Remembrance of Things Past, 1913-1927

There is not a woman in the world the possession of whom is as precious as that of the truth which
she reveals to us by causing us to suffer.

Marcel Proust
Remembrance of Things Past, 1913-1927

There is a relationship between the capacity of
a being to love, and its capacity to suffer, regardless
of its species. If a being, of whatever species, has the
capacity to give and receive love, then certainly it
will suffer if that capacity is thwarted. This is one of
the reasons all the wisdom traditions of the world
teach us that a sure way to make yourself miserable
is not to express your love.

John Robbins
Diet for a New America, 1987

Support and Love

To love means to communicate to the other that
you are all for him; that you will never fail him or
let him down when he needs you, but that you will
always be standing by with all the necessary encour-
agements. It is something one can communicate to
another only if one has it.

Ashley Montagu
The Cultured Man, 1958

Sweetness and Love

All love is sweet, given or returned. . . .
Those who inspire it most are fortunate. . . .
But those who feel it most are happier still.

Percy Bysshe Shelley

Talking and Love

Love is a talkative passion.

Bishop Wilson

Speak low if you speak love.

William Shakespeare
Much Ado About Nothing, 1598

Love's best habit is a soothing tongue.

William Shakespeare
The Passionate Pilgrim, 1599

Love is the silent saying and saying of a single name.

Mignon McLaughlin
The Neurotic's Notebook, 1963

To speak of love is to make love.

Honore de Balzac
As quoted in *The Wisdom of Balzac,* 1923

The music that can deepest reach,
And cure all ill, is cordial speech.

Ralph Waldo Emerson

You don't love a woman for what she says, but love what she says because you love her.

Andre Maurois

Tests of Love

The first test of love is that it knows no bargain. So long as you see a man love another to get something, you may know that is shopkeeper's love. Wherever there is any question of buying and selling, it is no longer love. So when any man is praying to God:

"Give me this and give me that," it is not love. How can it be? I offer you a prayer and you give me something in return; that is what it is, mere shopkeeping.

The second test is that love knows no fear. How can there be any fright in love? Does the lamb love the lion? The mouse the cat? The slave the master?

Slaves sometimes simulate love. But is it love? Where do you ever see love and fear? It is always a sham. So long as man thinks of God as sitting above the clouds with a reward in one hand and punishment in the other, there can be no love. . . .

The third is still a higher test. Love is always the highest ideal. The strongest and most attractive love is that between man and woman, and therefore that language was used in expressing the deepest devotion. The madness of this human love is the faintest echo of the mad love of the saints for God.

Swami Vivekananda
Religion of Love

Time and Love

Love vanquishes time. To lovers, a moment can be eternity, eternity can be the tick of a clock. Across the barriers of time and the ultimate destiny, love persists, for the home of the beloved, absent or present, is always in the mind and heart. Absence does not diminish love.

Mary Parrish

The richest love is that which submits to the arbitration of time.

Laurence Durrell

Love makes time pass. Time makes love pass.

French proverb

Time, which strengthens friendship, weakens love.

Jean De La Bruyere
Characters, 1688

Only in a continuing relationship is there a possibility for love to become deeper and fuller so that it envelops all our life and extends into the community.

Herbert Otto

I know a lot of people didn't expect our relationship to last -- but we've just celebrated our two months anniversary.

Britt Ekland

Love seems the swiftest, but it is the slowest of growths. No man or woman really knows what perfect love is until they have been married a quarter of a century.

Mark Twain

There are those who want to set fire to our world,
We are in danger,
There is only time to work slowly,
There is no time not to love.

Deena Metzger

Toast to Love

When the husband drinks to the wife, all would
be well; when the wife drinks to the husband, all is.

English proverb

Triangles and Love

Most of these love triangles are wrecktangles.

Anonymous

True Love

We don't believe in rheumatism and true love until after the first attack.

Marie von Ebner-Eschenbach

Those who have both true love and true friendship have received the highest gift God can offer.

Anonymous

A woman whom we truly love is a religion.

Emil De Giradin

True love is like a ghost; everyone talks of it, few have seen it.

Francois de La Rochefoucauld
Maxims, 1665

Unconditional Love

If we cannot love unconditionally, love is already in a critical condition.

Johann Wolfgang von Goethe

Evaluating and being evaluated by others, a habit from the past, results at worst in fear and at best in conditional love. To experience unconditional love, we must get rid of the evaluator part of ourself. In place of the evaluator, we need to hear our strong inner voice saying to ourselves and others, "I totally love and accept you as you are."

Gerald G. Jampolsky
Love is Letting Go of Fear, 1979

Unconditional love gives a stable foundation to a relationship. And it means just what it says. No conditions ---- no strings attached to my love. No matter what you say or do, I will continue loving you. I may not like what you do, but my love is unconditional and will not be affected ---- not even if our involvement changes.

Ken Keyes, Jr.
A Conscious Person's Guide to Relationships, 1979

Unconditional love is the most powerful stimulant to the immune system.

Bernie S. Siegal
Love, Medicine and Miracles, 1986

Unreciprocated Love

Love unreciprocated is like a question without an answer.

Kathryn Maye

The love that lasts longest is the love that is never returned.

W. Somerset Maugham

Valuation and Love

. . . I see little difference between love and valuation when taken in a practical way. I say that valuation is love; and I say also that if you say you love a person and do not value that person it is not love.

Maurice Nicoll
*Psychological Commentaries on the Teachings
of Gurdjieff and Ouspensky,* Volume 2 (1952)

Vitality and Love

The cure for all the ills and wrongs, the cares, the sorrows, and the crimes of humanity, all lie in that one word "love." It is the divine vitality that everywhere produces and restores life. To each and every one of us, it gives the power of working miracles if we will.

Lydia M. Child

The real value of love is the increased general vitality it produces.

Paul Valery

Vulnerability and Love

It seems that it is madder never to abandon one's self than often to be infatuated; better to be wounded, a captive and a slave, than always to walk in armor.

Margaret Fuller
Summer on the Lakes, 1844

Love is not love until love's vulnerable.

Theodore Roethke
The Collected Verse of Theodore Roethke, 1961

Men are taught that woman respect them for their strength and that may well be true, but they love them for their vulnerability.

Merle Shain
Some Men Are More Perfect Than Others, 1973

Vulnerability is always at the heart of love.

Leo Buscaglia
Love, 1972

Way to Love

The way to love anything is to realize that it might be lost.

G. K. Chesterton

Will and Love

Love is as love does. Love is an act of will ---- namely, both an intention and an action.

> M. Scott Peck
> *The Road Less Traveled,* 1978

There is no love where there is no will.

> Mohandas Gandhi

Sexual passion is the cause of war and the end of peace, the basis of what is serious, and the aim of the jest, the inexhaustible source of wit, the key to all allusions, and the meaning of all mysterious hints. . . just because the profoundest seriousness lies at its foundation. . . . But all this agrees with the fact that the sexual passion is the kernel of the will to live, and consequently the concentration of all desire; therefore in the text I have called the genital organs the focus of will.

> Arthur Schopenhauer

Winning and Losing Love

It is better to have loved and lost, than never to have loved at all.

Alfred Tennyson

To love and win is the best thing, to love and lose the next best.

William M. Thackeray

Though she on whom your heart is set is not for you, you are the richer for the fact that she exists. Thus, too, with the pearl at the bottom of the sea.

Antoine de Saint-Exupery
The Wisdom of the Sands, 1950

Love is never lost. If not reciprocated it will flow back and soften and purify the heart

Washington Irving

If you believe yourself unfortunate, because you have loved and lost, perish the thought. One who has loved truly, can never lose entirely. Love is whimsical and temperamental. It comes when it pleases, and goes away without warning. Accept and enjoy it while it remains, but spend no time worrying about its departure. Worry will never bring it back.

Napoleon Hill
Think and Grow Rich, 1937

What is defeat? Nothing but education, nothing but the first step to something better.

Wendell Phillips

Every man's got to figure to get beat sometime.

Joe Louis

What seem to us bitter trials are often blessings in disguise.

Oscar Wilde
The Importance of Being Earnest, 1899

Nothing happens to any man which he is not formed by nature to bear.

Marcus Aurelius

You must be present to win.

(Announcement usually made at bingo games and raffles)

Wisdom and Love

It is impossible to love and be wise.

Francis Bacon
Essays, 1825

In wise love each divines the high secret self of the other, and refusing to believe in the mere daily self, creates a mirror where the lover or the beloved sees an image to copy in daily life.

William Butler Yeats

Wishes and Love

When you love someone all your saved-up wishes start coming out.

Elizabeth Bowen
The Death of the Heart, 1938

Wives and Love

The test of a happily married, and a wise, woman is whether she can say, "I love you," far oftener than she asks, "Do you love me?"

Dorothy Dayton

Women and Love

The treasures of the deep are not so precious as are the concealed comforts of a man locked up in woman's love.

Thomas Middleton

Don't tell a woman she's pretty; tell her there is no other woman like her, and all roads will open to you.

Jules Renard

The knowledge of a man's countenance is, to the woman who loves him, like that of the sea to a sailor.

Honore de Balzac
As quoted in *The Wisdom of Balzac,* 1923

Woman would be more charming if one could fall into her arms without falling into her hands.

Ambrose Bierce

Women generally yield through weakness rather than through passion. Thus it is that enterprising men generally succeed better than others, although they may not be the most amiable.

Francois de La Rochefoucauld
Maxims, 1665

Love and respect woman. Look to her not only for comfort, but for strength and inspiration and the doubling of your intellectual and moral powers. Blot out from your mind any idea of superiority; you have none.

Joseph Mazzini

It is not as difficult to find a woman who has never been guilty of an indiscretion, as to find a woman who has been guilty of only one.

Francois de La Rochefoucauld
Maxims, 1665

There are a few things that never go out of style, and a feminine woman is one of them.

Ralston

Heaven preserve women from handsome men of promise!

Honore de Balzac
As quoted in *The Wisdom of Balzac,* 1923

No matter how happily a woman may be married, it always pleases her to discover that there is a nice man who wishes she were not.

H. L. Mencken

To a woman there is something indescribably inviting in a man whom other women favor.

Honore de Balzac
As quoted in *The Wisdom of Balzac,* 1923

Women who are in love forgive grave infidelities more than petty indiscretions.

Francois de La Rochefoucauld
Maxims, 1665

Woman's virtue is man's greatest invention.

Cornelia Otis Skinner

Work and Love

If you want to be happy for an hour, make love to the person you most desire; if you want to be happy for several hours eat a meal of all the foods you love, prepared just the way you like them; if you want to be happy for the rest of your life, love your work.

Chinese proverb

The love you liberate in your work is the only love you keep.

Elbert Hubbard

You have a right to work, but for work's sake only. You have no right to work for the fruits of work. They who work selfishly for results are miserable.

Bhagavad Gita

When love and skill work together, expect a masterpiece.

John Ruskin

A man's health seldom suffers from the work he loves and does for its own sake.

Honore de Balzac
As quoted in *The Wisdom of Balzac,* 1923

If a man loves to labor at any trade, apart from any question of success or fame, the gods have called him.

Robert Louis Stevenson

The return from your work must be the satisfaction which that work brings you and the world's need of that work. With this, life is heaven, or as near heaven as you can get. Without this ---- with work which you despise, which bores you, and which the world does not need ---- this life is hell.

William Edward Burghardt DuBois

The crowning fortune of a man is to be born to some pursuit which finds him employment and happiness, whether it be to make baskets, or broadswords, or candles, or statues, or songs.

Ralph Waldo Emerson

Had I followed my pleasure and chosen what I plainly have a decided talent for ---- police spy ---- I should have been much happier than I afterwards became.

Soren Kierkegaard

Doing what you love is an expression of your talent. Your talent and creativity are two gifts which have been given to you as an expression of the abundance of the Universe. When used in conjunction with each other, there is no limit to the further abundance you can create for yourself.

Arnold M. Patent
You Can Have It All, 1984

For one human being to love another: that is perhaps the most difficult of all our tasks, the ultimate, the last test and proof, the work for which all other work is but preparation.

Rainer Maria Rilke
Letters to a Young Poet, 1904

Worthiness and Love

The only love worthy of the name, ever and always uplifts.

George MacDonald

Wounds and Love

Next to the wound, what women make best is the bandage.

Barley

AUTHOR INDEX

NOTE: Next to the name of each author for whom it was possible to locate information is a short biographical sketch.

ABBOTT, Lyman (1835-1922; American clergyman, author)
 Patience and Love
ABHEDANANDA, Swami (1866-1939; disciple of Ramakrishna, lived in America for 30 years)
 Meanings of Love
ADE, George (1866-1944; American humorist)
 Elopement and Love
ADDISON, Joseph (1672-1719; English essayist, poet)
 Friendship and Love; Respect and Love
ALLEN, Woody (b. 1935; American comedian, director, writer, actor)
 Sex and Love
AMORY, Cleveland (b. 1917; American social historian, journalist, novelist)
 Marriage Proposals and Love
ANDERSON, Margaret
 Romantic Love
ANDERSON, Walter (b. 1944; American editor of *Parade Magazine*, author)
 Friendship and Love
ARISTOTLE (384-322 BCE; Greek philosopher)
 Friendship and Love
AUDEN, W. H. (1907-1973; American [English-born] poet)
 Humor and Love
AURELIUS, Marcus (121-180 AD; Roman emperor)
 Life and Love; Winning and Losing Love
BACON, Francis (1561-1626; English philosopher)
 Wisdom and Love
BAILEY, Pearl (1918-1990; American singer, entertainer)
 Ambition and Love

BALZAC, Honore de (1799-1850; French novelist, writer)
Age and Love; Eternity and Love; Fate and Love; Hatred and Love; Home and Love; Husbands and Love; Illusions and Love; Judging Love; Men and Love; Money and Love; Passion and Love; Reason and Love; Sex and Love; Talking and Love; Women and Love; Work and Love
BEAL, Louise (1867(?)-1952; actress)
Neighborly Love
BEAUVOIR, Simone de (1908-1986; French author)
Husbands and Love
BENSON, E. F. (1867-1940; English writer)
Blindness and Love
BIERCE, Ambrose (1842-1914 (?); American author)
Women and Love
BLACK, Beth
Looking for Love
BOGAN, Louise (1897-1970; American poet)
Poetry and Love
BORGES, Jorge Luis (1899-1988; Argentinean author)
God and Love
BOSSUET, Jacques (1627-1704; French bishop)
Reason and Love
BOSWELL, James (1740-1795; Scottish lawyer, author)
Second Love
BOWEN, Elizabeth (1899-1973; Anglo-Irish writer)
Jealousy and Love, Wishes and Love
BRADLY
Satisfaction and Love
BRICKNER, Barnett Robert (1892-1958; American rabbi)
Success in Love
BROUN, Heywood Campbell (1888-1939; American columnist)
Frivolous Love
BROWNING, Elizabeth Barrett (1806-1861; British poet)
Belief and Love
BUCK, Pearl S. (1892-1973; American novelist)
Death and Love

BUDDHA (563(?)-483(?) BC; Indian philosopher; founder of Buddhism)
　　Possessions and Love
BUSCAGLIA, Leo (born 1924; American teacher, author)
　　Completeness and Love; Falling in Love; Giving Love; Vulnerability and Love
BUTLER, Samuel (1835-1902; English novelist, satirist)
　　Reason and Love
BUTTERWORTH, Eric (20th-century American minister, author)
　　Health and Love, Learning to Love; Loneliness and Love; Self-love
BYRD, Richard E. (1888-1957; admiral, U.S. Navy; polar explorer)
　　Affection and Love
CAMPBELL, Joseph (1904-1987; mythologist, teacher, author)
　　God and Love
CAMPBELL, Ross (b. 1936; American psychiatrist, author)
　　Children and Love; Husbands and Love
CARNEGIE, Dale (1888-1955; lecturer, author, teacher of public speaking)
　　Beauty and Love
CHAMFORT, S. R. N. (1741-1794; French writer, wit)
　　Exaggeration and Love; Fantasy and Love; Mystery and Love
CHANG, Jolan (20th-century author)
　　Health and Love; Loving and Being Loved
CHAPMAN, George (1559(?)-1634; English dramatist, translator)
　　Love at First Sight
CHEKHOV, Anton (1860-1904; Russian dramatist, writer)
　　Loneliness and Love
CHER (b. 1946; American actress, singer)
　　Age and Love
CHESTERTON, G. K. (1874-1936; English journalist, author)
　　Enemies and Love; Sex and Love; Way to Love
CHEVALIER, Maurice (1888-1972; French movie star, entertainer)
　　Falling in Love
CHILD, Lydia M. (1802-1890; American abolitionist, novelist)
　　Vitality and Love

CHINMAYAANANDA, Swami (b. 1916; Indian spiritual teacher)
    Gifts and Love; Sacrifice and Love
CHURCHILL, Winston (1874-1965; British statesman, writer)
    Brilliant Achievement and Love
CIARDI, John (1916-1986; American poet)
    Age and Love
CICERO, (104-43 BC; Roman statesman, orator, author)
    Friendship and Love
CLOSE, Henry T. (American pastoral counselor; director of the
Milton Erickson Institute of Atlanta, Georgia)
    Parenting and Love
COBBETT, William (1763-1835; British political writer)
    Children and Love
COLERIDGE, Samuel Taylor (1772-1834; English poet)
    Happiness and Love
COLETTE (1873-1954; French actress)
    Life and Love
COLTON
    Punishment and Love
COLTS
    Attraction and Love
CONNOLLY, Cyril (1903-1974; English critic, author)
    Food and Love; Friendship and Love; Health and Love; Love
    Affairs and Love; Marriage and Love
CORELLI, Marie (1855-1924; English writer)
    Marriage and Love
COUDERT, Jo (b. 1923; American editor, author)
    Arithmetic and Love; Children and Love; Companionship
    and Love; Divorce and Love; Self-esteem and Love; Self-love
CROTS, Roy
    Self-improvement and Love
CULLEN, Countee (1903-1946; American poet, teacher)
    Death and Love
D'AUREVILLY, Barley
    Wounds and Love
DARROW, Clarence (1857-1938; American lawyer, author)
    Children and Love

DAUDET, Alphonse (1840-1897; French novelist)
    Ideal Love
DAVIS, Bette (1910-1993; American Actress)
    Children and Love; Life and Love
DAVIS, D.H.
    Blindness and Love
DAYTON, Dorothy (20th-century American writer)
    Wives and Love
de BEAUMARCHAIS, P.A.C. (1732-1799; French dramatist, man of affairs)
    Possessions and Love
DENVER, John (1943-1997; American songwriter, singer)
    Food and Love
DeVRIES, Peter (1910-1993; American writer and editor)
    Sex and Love
DEWAR, Thomas Robert (1864-1930; English [Scottish-born] distiller, sportsman, raconteur, author)
    Money and Love
DICKENS, Charles (1812-1870; British novelist)
    Affection and Love; Mystery and Love
DIETRICH, Marlene (1901-1992; German actress, singer)
    Grumbling and Love
DILLER, Phyllis (b. 1917; American comedienne)
    Success in Love
DISRAELI, Benjamin (1804-1881; British prime minister, author)
    First Love; Respect and Love; Success in Love
DOSTOEVSKY, Fyodor (1821-1881; Russian novelist)
    Happiness and Love; Simplicity of Love
DREY, Alexander
    Courtship and Love
DRYDEN, John (1631-1700; English poet, dramatist)
    Jealousy and Love; Reward of Love
DuBOIS, William Edward Burghardt (1868-1963; American educator, editor, writer)
    Work and Love
DURRELL, Laurence (1912-1990; Anglo-Irish novelist, poet, playwright)
    Time and Love

DYER, Wayne W. (b. 1940; American psychologist, novelist, author)
Giving Love; Meanings of Love
EBNER-ESCHENBACH, Marie von (1830-1916; baroness)
True Love
EKLAND, Britt (Swedish screen actress)
Time and Love
ELIOT, George (1819-1880; female English novelist)
Expectations and Love; Friendship and Love; Humor and Love
EMERSON, Ralph Waldo (1803-1882; American essayist, poet)
Affection and Love; Arithmetic and Love; Beauty and Love; The Eye and Love; Friendship and Love; Marriage and Love; Pleasure and Love; Relatives and Love; Talking and Love; Work and Love.
EURIPIDES (480(?)-406(?) BC; Greek dramatist)
Eternity and Love; Help and Love
FEY, Imogene; (American writer, contemporary)
Children and Love
FITZGERALD, F. Scott (1896-1940; American novelist; short story writer, playwright)
Kissing and Love
FOSDICK, Harry Emerson (1878-1969, American minister)
Bitterness and Love
FRANCIS, Brendan
Sex and Love
FRANKL, Viktor E. (1905-1997; Austrian psychotherapist, philosopher; founder of logotherapy [finding the meaning of one's life])
Importance of Love
FRANKLIN, Benjamin (1706-1790; American statesman, scientist, philosopher, businessman)
Marriage and Love; Success in Love
FREUD, Sigmund (1856-1939; Austrian neurologist; founder of psychoanalysis)
Death and Love; The Human Psyche and Love
FRIEDAN, Betty (b. 1921; American writer-feminist)
Dependence and Love

FRIEDMAN, Gil (b. 1935; American writer)

Books and Love, Dancing and Love, Flowers and Love, Forgiveness and Love, Friendship and Love, Lust vs. Love, Success and Love

FROMM, Erich (1900-1980; American [German-born] psychoanalyst)

Attitude and Love; Concern and Love; Existence and Love; Expectations and Love; Motherly Love

FROST, Robert (1874-1963; American poet)

Food and Love

FULLER, Margaret (1810-1850; American writer, philosopher)

Vulnerability and Love

FULLER, Thomas (1608-1661; English clergyman, author)

Knowing Your Lover; Marriage and Love; Pleasure and Love

GABOR, Zsa Zsa (b. 1919; Hungarian-born actress, married eight times)

Divorce and Love; Husbands and Love; Marriage and Love; Sex and Love

GANDHI, Mohandas (1869-1948; Indian national leader)

Sin and Love; Will and Love

GARCIA MARQUEZ, Gabriel (b. 1928; Colombian novelist, short story writer)

Age and Love

GARNER, James (b. 1928; American screen star)

Marriage and Love

GAUTIER, Theophile (1811-1872; French author)

Admiration and Love

GAWAIN, Shakti (b. 1948; American author)

Reflection and Love

GERALDY, Paul (1885-1983; French poet, playwright)

Choice and Love; Secret Love

GERARDIO, Madame de

Mutual Love

GIBRAN, Kahlil (1883-1931; Lebanese novelist, poet, artist, lived in U.S.)
>Death and Love; Direction and Love; Emptiness and Love; Happiness and Love; Kindness and Love; Loving and Being Loved; Passion and Love; Proximity and Love; Solitude and Love

GIRADIN, Emile de (1801-1886; French journalist)
>True Love

GIRAUDOUX, Jean (1882-1944; French writer)
>Death and Love

GLYN, Elinor (1864-1943; English novelist)
>Romance and Love

GOETHE, Johann Wolfgang von (1749-1832; German poet, dramatist, novelist, writer)
>Celebration of Love; Domination and Love; Friendship and Love; Influence of Love; Life and Love; Marriage and Love; Unconditional Love

GOLDSMITH, Warren H.
>Marriage and Love

GORDEN, Julius (American rabbi)
>Blindness and Love

GOURMONT, Remy de (1958-1915, French writer)
>Education and Love

GRACE, George W. (American psychologist)
>Proper Motions and Love

GRAHAM, Martha (1894-1991; American dancer and choreographer)
>Dancing and Love

GREENE, Graham (1904-1991; English novelist)
>Companionship and Love; Loving and Being Loved

GUEVARA, Che (1928-1967; physician, Marxist revolutionary leader, author)
>Revolution and Love

HADEWIJCH of ANTWERP (1200(?)-1250; female Dutch mystic, poet)
>Karma and Love; Service and Love

HALIFAX (1881-1959; English statesman, dramatist)
>Children and Love; Faults and Love

HAWTHORNE, Nathaniel (1804-1864; American author)
Passion and Love
HAY, Louise L. (b. 1935; American author, therapist, lecturer)
Self-love
HAZLITT, William (1778-1830; English essayist)
Love at First Sight
HERRICK, Robert
The Eye and Love
HESSE, Hermann (1877-1962; German novelist; lived in Switzerland)
Love and Loving
HILL, Napoleon (1883-1970; American author)
Winning and Losing Love
HODGES, Job E.
Jealously and Love
HOFFENSTEIN, Samuel (1890-1947; American poet, humorist, newspaperman, screen writer)
Marriage and Love
HOLMES, Jr., Oliver Wendell (1841-1935; lawyer, jurist, writer)
Age and Love
HOLMES, Sr., Oliver Wendell (1809-1894; physician, teacher, poet, essayist, novelist)
Methods of Love
HOMER (850(?) BC; traditional Greek epic poet)
Mutual Love
HOPKINS, Arthur (1878-1950; producer, playwright)
Death and Love
HOWE, Ed (1853-1937; American newspaperman, editor, humorist)
Divorce and Love; Exaggeration and Love
Howell, James (1594(?)-1666; Welsh author)
Faults and Love
HOWES, Barbara (1914-1996; American literary editor, poet)
Roots of Love
HUBBARD, Frank McKinney (1868-1930; American caricature artist)
Courtship and Love

HUBBARD, Elbert (1856-1915; American businessman, editor, biographer)
>Friendship and Love; Work and Love
HUGO, Victor (1802-1885; French poet, novelist, dramatist)
>Life and Love
HUXLEY, Aldous (1894-1963; English novelist, critic)
>Meanings of Love
IRVING, Washington (1783-1859; essayist, historian, biographer, humorist)
>Winning and Losing Love
JACKSON, Glenda (b. 1936; British actress)
>Sex and Love
JACKSON, Shirley (American novelist, 1920-1965)
>Relatives and Love
JAMES, Jennifer (American psychologist, newspaper columnist, author)
>Friendship and Love; Forgiveness and Love; Presents and Love
James, William (1842-1910; American psychologist, philosopher)
>Friendship and Love; Success in Love
JAMPOLSKY, Gerald G. (b. 1925; American psychiatrist, author; founder of Center for Attitudinal Healing)
>Fear and Love; Unconditional Love
JARSON
>Forgetfulness and Love
JEFFERS, Susan (b. 1938; American psychologist, author)
>Giving and Love; Patience and Love
JEFFERSON, Thomas (1743-1826; third president of the of U.S., 1801-1809)
>Friendship and Love
JEROME, Jerome K. (1859-1927; English humorist, novelist, playwright)
>Affection and Love
JERROLD, Douglas William (1803-1857; English playwright, humorist)
>Need to Love
JOHNSON, Robert A. (b. 1921; American Jungian analyst, author)
>Romantic Love

JOHNSON, Samuel (1709-1784; English author)
>Forgiveness and Love; Happiness and Love; Marriage and Love; Second Love

JONES, Franklin P.
>Life and Love

JONG, Erica (b. 1942; American novelist)
>Beauty and Love

JOUBERT, Joseph (1754-1824, French essayist, moralist)
>Success in Love

KARR, Jean Baptise Alphonse (1808-1890; French journalist, novelist)
>Expression of Love

KATZ, Mort
>Sex and Love

KATZ, Stan J. (b. 1949; American psychologist, author)
>False Love; Friendship and Love; Learning to Love

KERR, J.P.
>Happiness and Love

KEYES, Jr., Ken (1921-1995; American author; founder of Ken Keyes College)
>Emotional Acceptance and Love; Giving Love; Importance of Love; Unconditional Love

KIERKEGAARD, Soren (1813-1855; Danish philosopher, theologian)
>Conjugal vs. Romantic Love; Duty to Love; Importance of Love; Work and Love

KING, Alan (b. 1927; American comedian; Broadway producer, actor, writer)
>Marriage and Love

KING, Jr., Martin Luther (1929-1968; American minister, civil rights leader)
>Revolution and Love

KINGMA, Daphne Rose (American therapist, poet, and author)
>Apologies and Love; Compliments and Love

LA BRUYERE, Jean de (1645-1696, French moralist, author)
>Aversion and Love; Beauty and Love; Embarrassment and Love; Happiness and Love; Mystery and Love; Patience and Love; Proximity and Love; Time and Love

LA ROCHEFOUCAULD, Francois de (1613-80; French moralist, writer)

> Admiration and Love; Ambition and Love; Decay of Love; Forgiveness and Love; Friendship and Love; Judging Love; Love Affairs and Love; Loving and Being Loved; Mistress and Love; Passion and Love; Remedy and Love; Revealing and Feigning Love; True Love; Women and Love

LAMARTINE, Alphonse de (1790-1869; French poet)

> Secret Love

LAMENNAIS, Robert de (1782-1854; French priest, poet)

> God and Love

LANDERS, Ann (b. 1918; American advice columnist)

> Infatuation vs. Love; Sex and Love; Success in Love

LASKOW, Leonard (American physician)

> Healing and Love

LEIBNITZ, Gottfried Wilhelm (1646-1716; German philosopher, mathematician)

> Happiness and Love

LENNON, John (1940-1980; songwriter, musician, member of The Beatles)

> Arithmetic and Love

LESSING, Doris (b. 1919; English novelist)

> Age and Love

LEVERSON, Ada (1865-1936; English novelist)

> Knowing Your Lover

LEWIS, C.S. (1898-1963; English novelist, essayist)

> Friendship and Love

LINCOLN, Abraham (1809-1865; sixteenth president of the U.S., 1861-1865)

> Happiness and Love

LIPMAN, Maureen (b. 1946; English actress, writer)

> Sex and Love

LIU, Aimee K. (b. 1953; American author)

> False Love; Friendship and Love; Learning to Love

LONGFELLOW, Henry Wadsworth (1807-1882; American poet)

> Mystery and Love

LOREN, Sophia (b. 1934; Italian film actress)

> Sex and Love

LOUIS, Joe (1914-1981; world heavyweight boxing champion 1937-1949)
>Winning and Losing Love

LOWELL, James Russell (1819-1891; American essayist, diplomat)
>Action and Love

LUCE, Clare Boothe (1903-1987; American writer, politician, diplomat)
>Jealousy and Love

MacDONALD, George (1824-1905; Scottish novelist, poet)
>Marriage and Love, Worthiness and Love

MACE, David M.
>Sex and Love

MAE
>Affection and Love

MAILER, Norman (b. 1923; American novelist, short story writer, critic)
>Sex and Love

MALONE, Patrick Thomas (b. 1919; American psychiatrist, author)
>Change and Love; Completion and Love; Expectations and Love; Parenting and Love

MALONE, Thomas Patrick (b. 1944; American psychiatrist, author)
>Change and Love; Completion and Love; Expectations and Love; Parenting and Love

MANNES, David (1866-1959; American musician, educator)
>Seduction and Love

MARLOWE, Christopher (1564-1593; English dramatist)
>Love at First Sight

MARSHALL, George N. (b. 1920; American biographer, author)
>Possessions and Love

MARX, Groucho (1890-1977; American comedian, entertainer)
>Age and Love

MASCALL
>Family and Love

MASLOW, Abraham (1908-1970; American psychologist, teacher, author)
>Death and Love

MAUGHAM, W. Somerset (1874-1965; British novelist, dramatist, short story writer)

Change and Love; Death and Love; Unreciprocated Love

MAUROIS, Andre (1885-1967; French biographer, novelist)

Marriage and Love; Talking and Love

MAY, Rollo (1909-1994; American psychologist, author)

Independence and Love; Indifference and Love

MAYE, Kathryn

Unreciprocated Love

MAZZINI, Joseph (?) Giuseppe, 1805-1872; Italian patriot, critic, author)

Women and Love

McCARTHY, Mary (1912-1989; American novelist, journalist, critic)

Sex and Love

McCARTNEY, Paul (b. 1942; English songwriter, musician, member of The Beatles)

Arithmetic and Love

McGEE, Molly (1897-1961; American Actress)

Flowers and Love

McGINLEY, Phyllis (1905-1978; American essayist, poet)

Half a Love

McKUEN, Rod (b. 1933; American poet, composer, singer)

Importance of Love

McLAUGHLIN, Mignon (20th-century American editor, short story writer, humorist)

Arithmetic and Love; Divorce and Love; Incapacity to Love; Loving and Being Loved; Marriage and Love; Money and Love; Second Love; Talking and Love

MEAD, Margaret (1901-1978; American anthropologist)

Companionship and Love

MEHER BABA (1894-1969; Indian spiritual teacher)

Pure Love; Source of Love

MENCKEN, H.L. (1880-1956; American editor)

Methods of Love; Women and Love

MEREDITH, George (1828-1909; British novelist, poet)

Beauty and Love

METZGER, Deena (b. 1936; American poet, novelist, healer)

Time and Love

MICHENER, James (1907-1997; American author)
    Self-love
MIDDLETON, Thomas (1580(?)-1627; English dramatist)
    Women and Love
MILLAY, Edna St. Vincent (1892-1950; American poet)
    Decay of Love; Life and Love
MILLER, Harlan
    Success in Love
MILTON, John (1608-1674; English poet)
    Mutual Love
MISTINGUETT (stage name of Jeanne Bourgeois; 1875(?)-1956; French singer and dancer)
    Kissing and Love
MITCHELL, Joni (b. 1943; American songwriter, singer, painter)
    Illusions and Love
MOLIERE (1622-1673, French dramatist, actor)
    Dancing and Love; Reason and Love
MONDERSTANN
    Affection and Love
MONTAGU, Ashley (b. 1905; American [English-born] scientist, author)
    Support and Love
MOZART, Wolfgang Amadeus (1756-1791; Austrian composer)
    Genius and Love
MULLER, Robert (b. 1923; Belgian, United Nations Assistant Secretary General for 38 years)
    Forgiveness and Love
NASH, Ogden (1902-1971, American poet)
    Children and Love
NATHAN, George Jean (1882-1958; American critic, playwright, author)
    Humor and Love
NICOLL, Maurice (1884-1953; English writer, student of Gurdjieff, Ouspensky and Jung)
    Happiness and Love; Valuation and Love
NICHOLSON, Harold
    Success in Love

NIETZSCHE, Friedrich Wilhelm (1844-1900; German philosopher, poet)

>Change and Love; Success in Love

NIN, Anais (1903-1977; American [French-born] author; kept lifetime diary)

>Alchemy and Love; Anxiety and Love; Friendship and Love; Incapacity to Love

OTTO, Herbert (b. 1922; American [German-born] mental health educator, author)

>Adventure and Love; Time and Love

OVID (43 BC-17 AD; Roman poet)

>Success in Love

PARKER, Dorothy (1893-1967; American writer, satirist, humorist)

>Friendship and Love; Lingerie and Love; Mystery and Love

PARRISH, Mary (b. 1905; pseudonym for Margaret Cousins; American writer)

>Time and Love

PATENT, Arnold M. (b. 1929; seminar leader, author)

>Work and Love

PECK, M. Scott (b. 1936; American psychiatrist, author)

>Choice and Love; Falling in Love; Meanings of Love; Pain and Love; Success in Love; Will and Love

PERSE, Saint-John (1887-1975; French diplomat and poet)

>Death and Love

PHILLIPS, Wendell (1811-1884; American orator, reformer)

>Winning and Losing Love

PIERRE, Jean

>Pain and Love

PLATO (427(?)-347 BC; Greek philosopher)

>God and Love

PRIESTLY, J.B. (1733-1804; English novelist and writer)

>Marriage and Love

PROUST, Marcel (1871-1922; French novelist)

>Choice and Love; Expectations and Love; Reason and Love; Suffering and Love

PUBLILIUS SYRUS ("The Syrian"; 1st century BC; Roman slave; a mime, known for his aphorisms)

>Anger and Love

RACINE, Jean (1639-1699; French dramatist)
Belief and Love
RAJNEESH, Bhagwan Shree (1931-1990; Indian teacher, author)
Meditation and Love
RAY, Randolph (American minister, author)
Kindness and Love
RAY, Sondra (b. 1941; American author)
Energy and Love
REIDY, Jeanne (b. 1933; American philosopher, teacher, author)
Affection and Love; Loving and Being Loved; Need to Love;
Peace and Love; Possessiveness and Love
REIK, Theodor (1888-1969; American poet)
Sex and Love
RENARD, Jules (1864-1910; French author)
Women and Love
REUBEN, David (b. 1933; American psychiatrist, author)
Marriage and Love
RICHTER, Jean Paul (1763-1825; German writer)
Anger and Love; Delicacy and Love; Food and Love
RILKE, Rainer Maria (1875-1926; German poet)
Essence of Love; Miracle of Love; Solitude and Love; Work
and Love
ROBBINS, John (American author, contemporary)
Suffering and Love
RODMAN, Frances
Courtship and Love
ROETHKE, Theodore (1908-1963; American poet)
Vulnerability and Love
ROGERS
Knowing Your Lover
ROMAN, Sanaya (American, channel for "Orin")
Anger and Love; Commitment and Love; Food and Love;
Jealousy and Love; Self-love; Strength and Love
ROSENSTOCK-HUESSY, Eugen (1888-1973; American [German-
born] educator, author)
Sex and Love

ROUSSEAU, Jean-Jacques (1712-1778; French philosopher, author, social reformer)
>Patience and Love
ROWLAND, Helen (1875-1950; American writer, humorist)
>Anger and Love; Honeymoon and Love; Knowing Your Lover; Marriage and Love
RUSKIN, John (1819-1900; English essayist, critic, reformer)
>Work and Love
RUSSELL, Bertrand (1872-1970; English mathematician, philosopher)
>Children and Love; Loneliness and Love; Sex and Love
ST. AUGUSTINE (354430; leader of early Christian church)
>Beauty and Love; Loving and Being Loved; Sex and Love
ST. BOULANGER, Helen P. (20th-century American writer)
>Marriage and Love
St.JOHNS, Adela Rogers (1894-1988; American writer)
>Husbands and Love
SAINT-EXUPERY, Antoine de (1900-1944; French author)
>Barriers to Love; Direction and Love; Suffering and Love; Winning and Losing Love
SANTAYANA, George (1863-1952; Spanish poet, essayist; lived in U.S. from age of nine on)
>Belief and Love; Friendship and Love; Patience and Love; Sacrifice and Love
SCAD
>Attraction and Love
SCHOPENHAUER, Arthur (1788-1860; German philosopher)
>Will and Love
SCHUMAN, Robert
>Looking for Love
SENECA (4 BC(?)-65 AD; Roman statesman, philosopher)
>Kindness and Love
SHAIN, Merle (1935-1989; Canadian author)
>Friendship and Love; Happiness and Love; Romantic Love; Sex and Love; Vulnerability and Love
SHAKESPEARE, William (1564-1616; English dramatist, poet)
>Love and Loving; Talking and Love

SHAW, George Bernard (1856-1950; English [Irish-born] playwright, critic, author)

>Beauty and Love; Children and Love; Exaggeration and Love; Marriage and Love; Sacrifice and Love

SHEEHY, Gail (b. 1937; American writer

>First Love

SHELLEY, Percy Bysshe (1792-1822; English poet)

>Sweetness and Love

SIDNEY, Philip (1554-1586; English poet, statesman, soldier)

>Expression of Love

SIEGEL, Bernie S. (b. 1932; American surgeon, author)

>Healing and Love; Unconditional Love

SIMONS, Joseph (b. 1933; American psychologist, teacher, author)

>Affection and Love; Loving and Being Loved; Need to Love; Peace and Love; Possessiveness and Love

SKINNER, Cornelia Otis (1901-1979; American actress, writer)

>Women and Love

SMITH, Alexander (1830-1867; Scottish poet)

>Death and Love

SMITH, Liz (American syndicated columnist)

>Friendship and Love

SOCRATES (470(?)-399 BC; Greek philosopher)

>Marriage and Love

SOPHOCLES (496(?)-406 BC; Greek dramatist)

>Life and Love; Pain and Love

SPINOZA, Baruch (1632-1677; Dutch [Spanish-born] philosopher)

>Hatred and Love

STANLEY, Arthur Penrhyn (1815-1881; English historian, biographer, cleric)

>Faults and Love

STEINEM, Gloria (b. 1934; American feminist writer and cofounder of *Ms.* magazine)

>Loneliness and Love

STENDHAL (1783-1842; French author)

>Hope and Love

STEVENSON, Robert Louis (1850-1894; Scottish author)

>Devotion and Love; Friendship and Love; Service and Love; Work and Love

STOWE, Harriet Beecher (1811-1896; American author)
> Children and Love; Relatives and Love; Shyness and Love

SWIFT, Jonathan (1667-1745; English (Irish-born] satirist)
> Passion and Love

TAGORE, Rabindranath (1861-1941; Indian poet-philosopher)
> Mystery and Love

TAYLOR, Jeremy (1613-1667; English prelate, author)
> Friendship and Love

TEMPLE, William (1628-1699; English statesman)
> Pleasure and Love

TENNYSON, Alfred (1809-1892; English poet)
> Winning and Losing Love

TERENCE (190(?)-159 BC; Roman dramatist)
> Advice on Love

TERESA, MOTHER (1910-1997; Yugoslavian-born of ethnic Albanian parents] Roman Catholic nun; founder of religious order in Calcutta, India-Missionaries of Charity)
> Kindness and Love; Service and Love

THACKERAY; William M. (1811-1863; English [Indian-born] novelist)
> Winning and Losing Love

THOREAU, Henry David (1817-1862; American writer)
> Life and Love; Remedy for Love

TILLICH, Paul (1886-1965; American [German-born] theologian)
> Strength and Love

TOLSTOY, Leo (1828-1910; Russian novelist and philosopher)
> Beauty and Love

TOLSTOY, Countess Sonya (1844-1919; Russian, wife of Leo Tolstoy)
> Dependence and Love

TOYNBEE, Arnold J. (1888-1975; English historian)
> Life and Love

TUCKER, Sophie (1894-1966; American vaudeville, nightclub entertainer)
> Age and Love

TWAIN, Mark (1835-1910; American writer)
> Children and Love; Joy and Love; Time and Love

TZU, Kuo
> Food and Love

UNAMUNO, Miguel de (1864-1936; Spanish philosopher, writer)
> Illusions and Love

USTINOV, Peter (b. 1921; English actor, director, author)
> Forgiveness and Love

Van BUREN, Abigail (b. 1918; American writer-columnist)
> Money and Love

Van HORNE, Harriet (1920-1998; American writer-columnist)
> Cooking and Love

VALERY, Paul (1871-1945; French poet, philosopher)
> Vitality and Love

VISSELL, Barry (b. 1946; American physician, teacher, author)
> Completion and Love; Learning to Love; Spirituality and Love

VISSELL, Joyce (b. 1946; American nurse, teacher, author)
> Completion and Love; Learning to Love; Spirituality and Love

VIVEKANANDA, Swami (1863-1902; disciple of Ramakrishna, established the Vedanta movement in America
> God and Love; Tests of Love

VOLTAIRE (1694-1778; French writer)
> Meanings of Love

VOZNESENSKY, Andrei (b. 1933; Russian poet)
> Revolution and Love

WAUGH, Evelyn (1903-1966; English novelist)
> Friendship and Love

WEEKES, Claire (20th-century Australian psychologist, author)
> Happiness and Love

WEST, Dame Rebecca (1892-1983; English writer)
> Common Sense and Love

WEST, Mae (1892-1980; American movie "siren")
> Beauty and Love

WEST, Uta (b. 1928; American [Polish-born] author)
> Existence and Love

WHARTON, Edith (1862-1937; American novelist)
> Falling in Love; Money and Love

WHEELIS, Allen (b. 1915; American psychoanalyst, author)
Change and Love
WILDE, Oscar (1854-1900; English [Irish-born] writer)
Children and Love; Courtship and Love; Education and Love; First Love; Forgiveness and Love; Loving and Being Loved; Money and Love; Self-love; Winning and Losing Love
WILDER, Thornton (1897-1975; American author)
Energy and Love; Life and Love
WILLIAMS, Bern (b. 1913; American humorist)
Courtship and Love; Marriage and Love; Money and Love; Motherly Love
WILLIAMS, Paul (b. 1948; American author; founder of *Crawdaddy,* the first American rock magazine)
Advice on Love
WILLIAMS, Tennessee (1911-1983; American dramatist)
Pleasure and Love
WILSON, Bishop
Talking and Love
WILSON, Mrs. Woodrow (born Edith Bolting Galt; 1872-1961; second wife of U.S. President Woodrow Wilson)
Marriage Proposals and Love
WILSON, Woodrow (1856-1924; 28th U. S. President, 1913-1921)
Service and Love
WORDSWORTH, William (1770-1850; English poet)
Kindness and Love
YATES, Douglas
Incapacity to Love
YEATS, William Butler (1865-1939; Irish poet, dramatist)
Wisdom and Love
YOGANANDA, Paramahansa (1893-1952; Indian spiritual teacher, author; lived in America from 1922 on)
Brotherly Love
ZANGWILL, Israel (1864-1926; English dramatist, novelist)
Love at First Sight
ZOLOTOW, Maurice (b. 1913; American author)
Education and Love

207

ORDER FORM

Love Notes: Quotations from the Heart, compiled by Gil Friedman @ $12.95

How to Be Totally Unhappy in a Peaceful World: A Complete Manual with Rules, Exercises, a Midterm and Final Exam by Gil Friedman @ $11.95

> This is the ultimate self-help book. Whereas other self-help books tell you what you should do, could do, might do, this book tell you what you do. It is cheaper than therapy and makes a great bathroom book. Thirty cartoons, four pages of comics by an internationally renowned cartoonist. It is a children's book for adults. It has been translated into Chinese, Spanish and Danish.
>
> "From the 'Acknowledgements' up front to the blurbs on the back cover, there are unexpected fits of laughter awaiting you in this clever little book. It is an extended parody on self-help books, human nature, and on our frenetic, outer-oriented consumer society... This wise, clever and exceedingly funny book is a gem at $11.95."
>
> —*Arcata (CA) Eye*

Name _____

Address _____

City _____ **State** _____ **ZIP** _____

How to Order

Internet: www.yarapress.com

By Phone: Call (800) 352-2873; Visa, MasterCard, and Discover accepted.

By Mail: Send check or money orders (U.S. funds only) to Yara Press, 1735 J Street, Arcata, CA 95521

Please send the following items. I understand that I may return any item for a full refund, no questions asked.

Quantity   Book Title   Total

_____

_____

Total of above items: $_____

$2.50 first item; 50 cents each addl. **Shipping:** $_____

(Canada add $3.00 per order; Foreign add $4.00)

California addresses add 7.25% **Sales Tax:** $_____

Grand Total: $_____